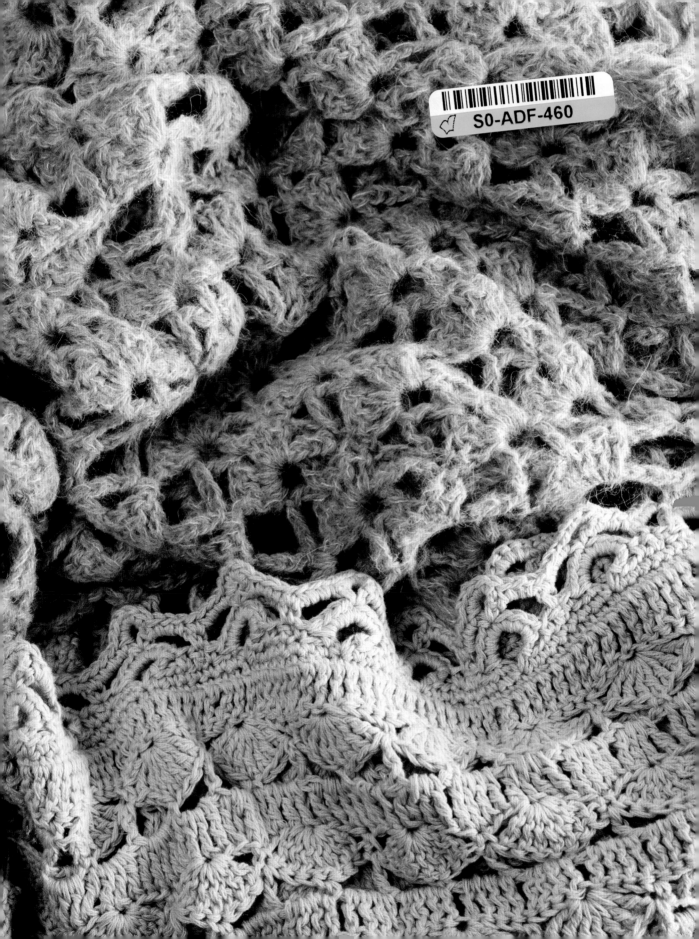

MAY BRITT BJELLA ZAMORI

Carefree Crochet

50 Soft, Fashionable Projects That Make You Feel Good

T
TRAFALGAR SQUARE
North Pomfret, Vermont

First published in the United States of
America in 2018 by
Trafalgar Square Books
North Pomfret, Vermont 05053

Originally published in Norwegian as *Hekling
i tykt og tynt.*

ISBN: 978-1-57076-888-0

Library of Congress Control Number:
2018932137

Photography: Guri Pfeifer
Charts: May Britt Bjella Zamori
Interior Design: Lise Mosveen
Cover Design: RM Didier
Translation into English: Carol Huebscher
Rhoades

Printed in China
10 9 8 7 6 5 4 3 2 1

CONTENTS

PREFACE

The original title of this book translates literally as "Crochet in Thick and Thin"—a title that obviously refers to crocheting with thick and thin yarns, but can also refer to a lifelong love of crochet.

I learned to knit when I was four or five years old, and learned to crochet a few years later. I remember going to a workshop with the older women in Øvre-Ål, Norway, early in the 1970s. All of my brown and orange swatches have been saved as proof!

At that time, most crochet patterns were for doilies, lace cuffs, and potholders. I'm sure many of my friends shook their heads when they opened Christmas gifts and found a crocheted doily from me. There's a limit to how many doilies a ten-year-old wants …

Fate brought me together with Tine Solheim. I began to test-knit her designs, and when it came out that I could also crochet, I was assigned to those projects as well. I quickly learned that there were all kinds of things to crochet besides doilies! This gave me the opportunity to learn more from Tine's work, and I absorbed everything she had to say about proportions, shaping, colors, and much more. I thought it was fantastic to enter this world full of creativity, colors, and textures, and the inspiration for this book began to grow.

The clothes in this book are designed to be worn! For the most part, these are everyday garments—but your styling and color choices can easily turn just about any design into lovely eveningwear (except perhaps the bikini!).

I've designed some easy garments and some that will probably take a little more experience to complete. I've also designed pillows, hats, and wrist warmers—it may be a good idea to start off with these small accessories, and then proceed to larger garments when you're confident you've mastered the patterns. At the same time, you'll have made something useful!

When I crochet gauge swatches, I work them as specified—and then, once I've measured them and confirmed that I can match the gauge, I keep going and turn them into small, practical items. For anyone who thinks swatches are wasted time and yarn, I recommend this approach.

Last autumn, I was sitting on a plane and crocheting. The woman in the seat next to me asked what I was making. I was crocheting the sleeve for a sweater, I told her. She wanted to know whether it was really possible to crochet a sweater. I confirmed that it was. And was it for an adult? Yes, it was. Then she shook her head and admitted that it did look good, but she just couldn't imagine a crocheted sweater…

I hope your imagination might reach a little further—that you can not only picture such a sweater, but that it could be the one you always sling over your shoulder on the way out the door, the one that goes with everything and is so soft you never want to take it off … and that you find that sweater in this book!

May Britt

Green Vest

It's always nice to have a lovely long vest to throw on! This one is crocheted in a fuzzy alpaca yarn. The yarn's available in a large range of colors, from delicate light blue to bright pink, so you don't have to use green—choose your favorite, and get started.

LEVEL OF DIFFICULTY
Intermediate

VEST
SIZES
S (M/L, L/XL, XXL)

FINISHED MEASUREMENTS
Chest: 39½ (45¼, 51¼, 57) in / 100 (115, 130, 145) cm
Length: 35½ (35½, 35½, 35½) in / 90 (90, 90, 90) cm
Back, width: approx. 19¾ (21¾, 25½, 27½) in / 50 (55, 65, 70) cm; the fronts overlap

HAT
SIZE
One size

FINISHED MEASUREMENTS
Circumference: 22 in / 56 cm

MATERIALS
Yarn: CYCA #4 (worsted/afghan/Aran) Du Store Alpakka Faerytale (100% alpaca, 191 yd/175 m / 50 g

Yarn Color and Amounts:
Green 744
Vest: 300 (350, 400, 450) g
Hat: 50 g

Crochet Hook: U.S. size H-8 / 5 mm + U.S. size G-6 / 4 mm for the edging on the hat

GAUGE
1 repeat over 8 ch in Pattern A with larger hook = approx. 2 in / 5 cm; 14 sts in Pattern B with larger hook = 4 in / 10 cm.
Adjust hook size to obtain correct gauge if necessary.

TECHNIQUES and PATTERNS
Treble crochet groups (tr gr): 4 treble crochet sts into the same st.

PATTERN A CROCHETED BACK AND FORTH (MULTIPLE OF 8 + 1 STS)

Row 1: Ch 1, 1 sc in 1st ch, (ch 2, skip 3 ch, 4 tr in next ch, ch 2, skip 3 ch, 1 sc in next ch) across.
Row 2: Ch 1, 1 sc in 1st sc, (ch 3, 1 sc between the 2 center tr in tr gr, ch 3, 1 sc in next sc) across.
Row 3: Ch 4 (=1st tr), 2 tr in 1st sc, (ch 2, 1 sc in next sc, ch 2, 4 tr in next sc) across ending with ch 2, 1 sc in next sc, ch 2, 3 tr in last sc.
Row 4: Ch 1, 1 sc in 1st tr, (ch 3, 1 sc in next sc, ch 3, 1 sc between the 2 center tr of tr gr) across. End with ch 3, 1 sc in next sc, ch 3, 1 sc in 4th ch at beg of previous row.
Row 5: Ch 1, 1 sc in 1st sc, (ch 2, 4 tr in next sc, ch 2, 1 sc in next sc) across.
Rep Rows 2-5.

PATTERN A CROCHETED IN THE ROUND (MULTIPLE OF 8 STS)

Rnd 1: Ch 1, (1 sc in 1st sc, ch 2, skip 3 sc, 4 tr in next ch, ch 2, skip 3 sc) around, ending with 1 sl st in 1st sc.
Rnd 2: Ch 1, 1 sc in 1st sc, (ch 3, 1 sc between the center 2 tr of tr gr, ch 3, 1 sc in next st) around, ending with ch 3, 1 sc between the center 2 tr of tr gr, ch 3, 1 sl st into 1st sc).
Rnd 3: Ch 4 (= 1st tr), 2 tr in 1st sc, (ch 2, 1 sc in next sc, ch 2, 4 tr in next sc) around, ending with ch 2, 1 sc in next sc, ch 2, 1 tr in last sc, 1 sl st into 4th ch at beg of rnd.
Rnd 4: Ch 1, 1 sc in space between the ch 4 and next tr, (ch 3, 1 sc in next st, ch 3, 1 sc between the 2 center tr of tr gr) around, ending with ch 3, 1 sc in next sc, ch 3, 1 sl st into 1st sc.
Rnd 5: Ch 1, 1 sc in 1st sc, (ch 2, 4 tr in next sc, ch 2, 1 sc in next sc) around, ending with ch 2, 4 tr in next sc, ch 2, 1 sl st into 1st sc.
Rep Rnds 2-5.

PATTERN B CROCHETED BACK AND FORTH

Row 1: Ch 3, 1 dc in each ch across row.
Row 2: Ch 3, 1 dc between the 1st and 2nd dc, 1 dc between each dc across row.
Rep Row 2.

PATTERN B CROCHETED IN THE ROUND

Work around in pattern as above, ending each rnd with 1 sl st into 3rd ch at beg of rnd.

TIPS FOR DECREASING

When decreasing at the beginning of a row, sl st over each of the sts you need to decrease. At the end of the row, turn before the sts which are to be decreased.

VEST

BACK

With larger hook, ch 81 (89, 97, 105). Work back and forth in Pattern A until piece measures approx. 23½ in / 60 cm; end with Row 2 of pattern.
Sleeve shaping: Increase 1 rep on each side on every other row 3 times, as shown on the chart. Pm at each side to mark beginning of armhole. Continue without further shaping until piece measures approx. 34 in / 86 cm. End with Row 3 of pattern.
Shoulder shaping: Decrease 2½ rep on each side 2 times as shown on the chart. At the left side, work sl st over the sts which are being eliminated, and, at the right side, turn, leaving rem sts unworked. The last row is a row ending with a ch-3 loop.

RIGHT FRONT

With larger hook, ch 25 (33, 41, 49). Work back and forth in Pattern A until piece measures approx. 23½ in / 60 cm; end with Row 2 of pattern. The front should be the same length as the back when you begin shaping the sleeves.
Sleeve and shoulder shaping: Increase and pm as for the left side of the back. Continue without further shaping until front is same length as back to shoulder shaping. Shape shoulder as for left side of back, ending on the same row in pattern.

LEFT FRONT

Work as for right front, reversing shaping to correspond. Increase for the sleeve and shape shoulder as for right side of the back.

FINISHING

Weave in all ends neatly on WS. Seam the sides beginning at lower edge and up to the marker for beginning of armhole. Seam shoulders.
Edging around the vest: Beginning at the right shoulder seam, work 1 rnd sc all around the outer edge of vest as follows: Along the back neck, work 2 sc over each ch loop and 1 sc into each sc. Along the front edges, work 3 sc around each tr / ch 4 and 1 sc in each sc. At the lower edge, work 3 sc over each ch loop, skip sc but work 1 sc in the same ch with the 4-tr gr; work 3 sc in each corner. Make the wide band to go around the fronts/neck separately. Ch 17. Beginning in the 3rd ch from hook, work Pattern B =

Pattern A crocheted back and forth

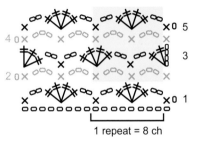

1 repeat = 8 ch

Increasing for the sleeves on each side of the back

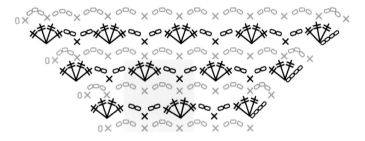

Shoulder shaping on the left side

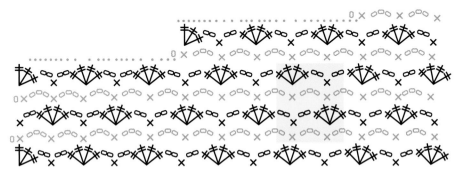

Pattern B crocheted back and forth

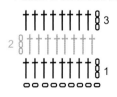

Chart Symbols

o = ch

x = sc

† = dc

‡ = tr

= 1 repeat

14 dc. Continue the band in Pattern B until it is approx. 79 in / 2 meters long. Sew or crochet the band securely along the front edges and back neck. Make sure it lies flat and smooth or the vest will pull in at the center front.

Armhole edging: Work around each armhole with sc as along the front edges. Then, ch 11. Beginning in the 3rd ch from hook, work Pattern B back and forth until the edging goes all around the sleeve. Do not make the edging too wide or it will flare out. Sew or crochet the edging securely around the sleeve edge.

9

HAT

With smaller hook, ch 72 and join into a ring with 1 sl st into 1st ch. Work Pattern B in the round until edging measures 5½ in / 14 cm. Change to larger hook.

Next Rnd: Ch 1 and then work 1 sc between each dc around; end with 1 sl st into 1st st.

Continue in Pattern A in the round for 8 in / 20 cm, ending on Rnd 2 or 4.

Next Rnd: Ch 1 and then work 1 sc in each sc, skipping ch loops around. Cut yarn, leaving a long end. Gather top sts; tighten and fasten off.

Attach yarn at lower edge on WS. Ch 1 and then work 1 sc between each dc, ending with 1 sl st into 1st sc. Cut yarn and fasten off; weave in all ends neatly on WS.

Fold lower edge up.

Beige Hat, Scarf, and Mittens

This set is crocheted with a heavy wool yarn so the accessories will look sturdy but, at the same time, will be quick and easy to crochet. The scarf is not very wide because of the thickness. It's crocheted lengthwise, so if you want a wider scarf you just have to crochet a couple of extra rows. The mittens are crocheted with a smaller hook size to firm up the pattern and make the mittens warmer.

LEVEL OF DIFFICULTY
Intermediate

SIZE
One size

FINISHED MEASUREMENTS
Hat: Circumference, approx. 21¼ in / 54 cm
Scarf: Width approx. 8 in / 20 cm; Length approx. 75 in / 190 cm + fringe
Mittens: Circumference approx. 8¾ in / 22 cm; desired length

MATERIALS
Yarn: CYCA #5 (bulky) Svarta Fåret Lovikka (100% wool, 65 yd/59 m / 100 g)

Yarn Color and Amounts:
Beige 7605
Mittens: 200 g
Hat: 200 g
Scarf: 700 g

Crochet Hook: U.S. size P / 12 mm for the hat and U.S. size J-10 / 6 mm for the mittens

GAUGE
1 repeat in Pattern A with larger hook = approx. 4¼ in / 11 cm.
Adjust hook size to obtain correct gauge if necessary.

TECHNIQUES
Double crochet group (dc gr): 4, 5, or 9 dc worked into the same stitch.
Double crochet cluster (dc cl): 4, 5, or 9 dc crocheted together.

PATTERN A CROCHETED BACK AND FORTH (MULTIPLE OF 8 + 1 STS)

Row 1: Ch 1, (1 sc, skip 3 sts, 9 dc in next st, skip 3 sts) across, ending with 1 sc in last st.

Row 2: Ch 3, skip 1st sc, 4-dc cl over next 4 dc, [ch 3, 1 sc in next dc (the center dc of the 9), ch 3, 9-dc cl over the next 4 dc + 1 sc + 4 dc] across, ending with 5-dc cl over the last 4 dc + last sc.

Row 3: Ch 3, 4 dc in top of 5-dc cl, (skip 3 ch, 1 sc in sc, skip 3 ch, 9 dc in top of 9-dc cl) across, ending with 5 dc in top of 4-dc cl at beg of previous row.

Row 4: Ch 1, 1 sc in 1st dc, ch 3, (9-dc cl over the next 4 dc + 1 sc + 4 dc, ch 3, 1 sc in next dc, ch 3) across, ending with 1 sc in 3rd ch at beg of previous row.

Row 5: Ch 1, 1 sc in 1st sc, (skip 3 ch, 9 dc in top of 9-dc cl, skip 3 ch, 1 sc in sc) across.

Rep Rows 2-5.

PATTERN A CROCHETED IN THE ROUND (MULTIPLE OF 8 STS)

Rnd 1: Ch 1, 1 sc in 1st ch, (skip 3 ch, 9 dc in next ch, skip 3 ch, 1 sc in next ch) around, ending with 1 sl st in 1st sc.

Rnd 2: Ch 3 (= 1st dc), skip 1st sc, 4-dc cl over next 4 dc, [ch 3, 1 sc in next dc (the center dc of the 9), ch 3, 9-dc cl over the next 4 dc + 1 sc + 4 dc] around, ending with 5-dc cl over the last 4 dc + last sc; end with 1 sl st in 3rd ch at beg of rnd.

Rnd 3: Ch 3, 4 dc in top of 5-dc cl, (skip 3 ch, 1 sc in sc, skip 3 ch, 9 dc in top of 9-dc cl) around, ending with 4 dc in top of 4-dc cl; end with 1 sl st into 3rd ch.

Rnd 4: Ch 4 (= 1st sc + ch 3), [9-dc cl over the next 4 dc + 1 sc + 4 dc, ch 3, 1 sc in next dc (the center of the 9 dc), ch 3] around, ending with 1 sl st in 4th ch at beg of rnd.

Rnd 5: Ch 1, 1 sc in 1st sc, (skip 3 ch, 9 dc in top of 9-dc cl, skip 3 ch, 1 sc in sc) around, ending with 1 sl st in 1st sc.

Rep Rnds 2-5.

PATTERN B CROCHETED IN THE ROUND (MULTIPLE OF 2 STS)

Rnd 1: Ch 1, 1 sc in 1st st, (ch 1, skip 1 st, 1 sc in next st) around.

Rnd 2: (1 sc around ch loop, ch 1, skip 1 sc) around.

Pattern A crocheted back and forth

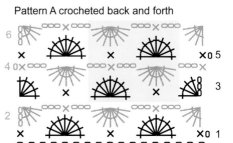

1 repeat = 8 ch

Pattern B crocheted in the round

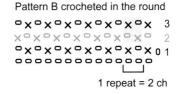

1 repeat = 2 ch

Chart Symbols

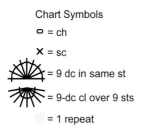

o = ch

✕ = sc

= 9 dc in same st

= 9-dc cl over 9 sts

= 1 repeat

Rep Rnd 2, working in a spiral = do *not* end rnds with 1 sl st into 1st st.

HAT

With larger hook, ch 40. Join into a ring with 1 sl st into 1st ch. Work 6 rnds of Pattern A in the round.
Rnd 7, top shaping: Ch 3, 2 dc in top of the 4-dc cl, (skip 3 ch, 1 sc in sc, skip 3 ch, 5 dc in top of the 9-dc cl) around, ending with 3 dc in top of the 5-dc cl, 1 sl st into 3rd ch.
Rnds 8-9: Ch 3, 2 dc tog over 2 dc around. End with 1 sl st into 3rd ch at beg of rnd.
Cut yarn, leaving a long end. Gather top sts; tighten and fasten off.
Attach yarn at bottom edge. Ch 1 and then work 3 sc over each ch loop around. On next rnd, work 1 sc in each sc, ending with 1 sl st into 1st sc. Weave in all ends neatly on WS.

SCARF

With larger hook, ch 129. Work 6 rows of Pattern A back and forth.
Turn the work and crochet along the short end. Ch 1 and then work 14 sc evenly spaced across; turn.
Ch 1, 1 sc in each sc. Rep the last row 5 more times.
Edge the opposite short end the same way.
Work 1 row of sc evenly spaced along each long edge. Weave in all ends neatly on WS.
Fringe: Cut 3 strands, 13¾ in / 35 cm long for every fringe. Fold each group. Use a rug knot to attach 8 fringes along each short end of the scarf.

MITTENS

With smaller hook, ch 25 and join into a ring with 1 sl st into 1st ch. Ch 1 and then work 1 sc in each ch around, ending with 1 sl st into 1st sc. Work 4 rnds of Pattern A in the round. Ch 1, 1 sc in each sc, 3 sc around each ch loop and 1 sc in each 9-dc cl and 1 sl st into 1st sc = 24 sc. Pm at the beginning of rnd (move up marker every rnd) and work 2 rnds of Pattern B but do *not* join rnds with sl st. On the next rnd, increase for the thumb gusset: work (1 sc, ch 1 and pm in this ch, 1 sc) around the same ch, move marker up every rnd. Increase the same way on every rnd 2 more times at the marked ch. On the next rnd, skip (ch before marker, the marked ch and the ch after marker) for the thumbhole. Continue in pattern until the mitten covers the ring finger. On the next rnd, work only 1 sc over each ch and do not ch between sc. Work (1 sc, skip 1 sc) until 3 sc rem. Cut yarn, gather sts at top; tighten and fasten off.
Thumb: Work in Pattern B around the thumbhole (1 sc, ch 1) 6 times on the 1st rnd. Work 5 rnds in pattern and then finish as for top of mitten. Weave in all ends neatly on WS.
Make both mittens the same way.

Fringed Bag

Who doesn't have an unused brooch lying around? I used one as a decoration to embellish this bag. If you want a closure, you can sew on a large snap or press button on the lower edge of the flap. I decided to make a shoulder strap out of a piece of leather recycled from an old bag, but the pattern gives the instructions for a crocheted strap—use whichever you like better!

LEVEL OF DIFFICULTY
Advanced

FINISHED MEASUREMENTS
Circumference: approx. 27½ in / 70 cm
Length: approx. 18¼ in / 46 cm

MATERIALS
Yarn: CYCA #4 (worsted/afghan/Aran) Garn Studio Drops Paris (100% cotton, 82 yd/75m / 50 g

Yarn Color and Amount:
Natural White 17: 450 g

Crochet Hook: U.S. size 7 / 4.5 mm

GAUGE
Approx. 19 sts in pattern = 4 in / 10 cm.
Adjust hook size to obtain correct gauge if necessary.

TECHNIQUES
Increasing: Work (1 sc, ch 1, 1 sc, ch 1) into same st.
Decreasing: Skip (1 sc, ch 1, 1 sc).
3-hdc cl: 3 hdc crocheted together
4-hdc cl: 4 hdc crocheted together

NOTE: Crochet the bag first. Work the netting and then the flower blocks for the flap. The two types of block are crocheted together and then joined with the bag.

BAG

Ch 42.

Rnd 1: Beginning in 2nd ch from hook, work (1 sc, ch 1) in each ch, with (1 sc, ch 1, 1 sc, ch 1) in last ch. Turn and work 1 sc, ch 1) in each ch along the other side of foundation chain. In the last ch, work (1 sc, ch 1). Pm in the center ch on each side and move marker up each rnd. Continue working around but do *not* join rnds with sl st; simply move marker to beg of rnd.

Rnd 2: Work (1 sc around ch, ch 1) around. *At the same time*, shape bag at the sides: see explanations on page 14.

Increase at each side on every other rnd 6 times. Continue as est until bag measures approx. 10¼ in / 26 cm. Now decrease at each side on every other rnd 6 times.

Next Rnd: Work 1 sc on each ch, skipping each sc.

Next Rnd: Work 1 sc in each sc, ending with 1 sl st into 1st sc to join. Cut yarn.

FLAP

Whole Netting Block (make 2 alike)

Ch 21.

Row 1: Beg in 3rd ch from hook, (= 1 hdc + ch 1), (skip 1 ch, 1 hdc around next ch, ch 1) 8 times. Work 1 hdc around last ch; turn.

Row 2: Ch 3 (= 1 hdc + ch 1), (1 hdc in next hdc, ch 1) 8 times; turn.

Rep Row 2 7 more times. There should be 9 "holes" vertically and horizontally. Do not cut yarn. Work 2 sc in each ch loop / around each hdc around the entire block, with 3 sc in each corner. End with 1 sl st into 1st sc.

Half Netting Block (make 2 alike)

Ch 21.

Row 1: Beg in 3rd ch from hook = 1st hdc + ch 1), (skip 1 ch, 1 hdc around next ch, ch 1) 8 times, end with 1 hdc around last ch; turn.

Row 2: 1 sl st each in 1st ch and next hdc, ch 3 (= 1st hdc + ch 1), (1 hdc in next hdc, ch 1) 7 times; turn.

Row 3: Ch 3, (1 hdc in next hdc, ch 1) 6 times; turn.

Rep Rows 2-3 6 more times with 1 "hole" less in each row. Do *not* cut yarn. Work 2 sc in each ch loop / around each hdc all around the block, with 3 sc in each corner; end with 1 sl st into 1st sc.

Flower block: Ch 6 and join into a ring with 1 sl st into 1st ch.

Rnd 1: Ch 4 (= 1 dc + ch 1), (1 dc around ring, ch 1) 11 times. End with 1 sl st into 3rd ch at beg of rnd = 12 dc.

Rnd 2: 1 sl st around next ch, ch 2, 3-hdc cl over the same ch, ch 2, 4-hdc cl around next ch, ch 3, [1 tr in next dc, ch 3, (4-hdc cl around next ch, ch 2) 2 times, 4-hdc cl around next ch, ch 3] 3 times, 1 tr in next dc, ch 3, 4-hdc cl around next ch, ch 2, 1 sl st in top of 1st hdc cl.

Rnd 3, joining: Ch 1, 1 sc in top of hdc-cl, ch 5, 1 sl st in 1st ch of the 5, ch 2, skip 2 ch + 1 hdc cl, 5 dc around next ch-3 loop, ch 1, 1 tr in tr, ch 3, 1 sl st in 1st ch of the 3, ch 1, 5 dc around next ch-3 loop, ch 2, skip 1 hdc cl + 2 ch, 1 sc in top of hdc cl, ch 5, 1 sl st in 1st ch of the 5, ch 2, skip 2 ch + 1 hdc cl, 5 dc around next ch-3 loop, ch 1, 1 tr in tr, (ch 1, 1 sl st in corner of a whole netting block, ch 1, 1 sl st in 1st ch, ch 1, 3 dc around next ch-3 loop, skip 3 sc of netting block, 1 sl st in next sc, 2 dc around the same ch loop, ch 2, skip 1 hdc cl + 2 ch, 1 sc in top of hdc cl, ch 2, skip 4 sc of netting block, 1 sl st in next sc, ch 2, 1 sl st in 1st ch, ch 2, skip 2 ch + 1 hdc cl, 2 dc around next ch-3 loop, skip 4 sc of netting block, 1 sl st in next sc, 3 dc around same ch loop, ch 1, 1 tr in tr) work and rep once more with the next whole netting block, ch 1, 1 sl st in corner of a whole netting block, ch 1, 1 sl st in 1st ch, ch 1, 5 dc around next ch-3 loop, ch 2, skip 1 hdc cl + 2 ch, 1 sc in top of hdc cl, ch 5, 1 sl st in 1st ch of the 5, ch 2, skip 2 ch + 1 hdc cl, 5 dc in next ch-3 loop, ch 1, 1 tr in tr, ch 3, 1 sl st in 1st ch of the 3, ch 1, 5 dc around next ch-3 loop, ch 2, 1 sl st into 1st sc.

Make 3 more blocks the same way, joining at the same time to whole and half netting blocks. See photo.

FINISHING

Flap: With RS facing, work 1 row sc along the right edge which will be joined to the bag. Lay the flap over the front of the bag and join the piece with sl st to the back from the RS of the work.

Shoulder strap: It can be difficult to find shoulder straps. Perhaps you have a bag at home with leather straps with clasps at each side. Attach the clasps to the bag or sew a ring on each side and attach the straps to them. You can also crochet a strap: Ch 12 and work rather firmly back and forth in sc, until the strap is desired length.

Fringe: Cut 6 strands, 12¾ in / 32 cm long for each of the 13 fringes. Fold each bundle in half and attach the fringe evenly across each side of the flap (see photo). Trim the fringe even and attach a brooch at the center of the bottom flower block.

Blue or Gray Hat and Wrist Warmers

If you don't want to go straight into making the pink jacket on page 42, you can try out the same pattern stitch, with raised double crochet stitches, on a hat or a pair of wrist warmers. You can also decide whether you want to top the hat with a pompom. (The gray version of the hat shown on page 42 sports a pompom, if you want to see what it might look like!)

LEVEL OF DIFFICULTY
Intermediate

SIZE
One size

FINISHED MEASUREMENTS
HAT
Circumference: approx. 19¾ in / 50 cm, but very elastic

WRIST WARMERS
Circumference: 8 in / 20 cm
Length: 8¼ in / 21 cm

MATERIALS
Yarn:
CYCA #3 (DK/light worsted), Du Store Alpakka Sterk (40% Merino wool, 40% alpaca, 20% polyamide, 150 yd/137 m / 50 g)

Yarn Color and Amount:
Gray 822 or Blue 815: 200 g

Crochet Hook: U.S. size G-6 / 4 mm

GAUGE
1 repeat over 10 ch in pattern = 2 in / 5 cm.
Adjust hook size to obtain correct gauge if necessary.

TIP
If you want to crochet a cowl with this pattern motif, begin with the same number of chain stitches as for the hat and work around until cowl is desired length.

NOTE: The pattern is explained in the text on page 44.

HAT

Ch 93. Work 24 rows back and forth in pattern (= end with 12th row of chart).

Row 25, shaping: Ch 3, (1 FPdc around each of next 3 dc, ch 2, 1 sc around the 2-ch loop, ch 2, 1 FPdc around each of next 3 dc) across, ending with ch 2, 1 sc around ch-2 loop, ch 2, 1 FPdc around each of next 3 dc, 1 hdc in 2nd ch at beg of previous row.

Row 26: Ch 1, 1 sc in hdc, ch 2, 1 FPdc around each of next 3 dc, (ch 2, 1 FPdc around each of next 6 dc) across. End with 1 FPdc around each of next 3 dc, ch 2, 1 sc in 2nd ch at beg of previous row.

Row 27: Ch 2, (2 FPdc tog over the next 2 dc, 1 FPdc in next dc) across.

Row 28: Ch 2 and then work (2 FPdc tog) across. Cut yarn and gather rem sts; tighten. Seam the hat at center back.

Edging: Attach yarn at lower edge of hat and work 1 sc in each dc, 1 sc in each ch loop, and in each sc around. Finish with a round of crab st (single crochet worked from left to right) and fasten off. Weave in all ends neatly on WS.

WRIST WARMERS
(make 2 alike)

Ch 41. Work 24 rows back and forth in pattern (= end with 12th row of chart).

Row 25: Ch 3, (1 FPdc around each of the next 3 dc, ch 2, 1 sc around ch-2 loop, ch 2, 1 FPdc around each of the next 3 dc) across, ending with ch 2, 1 sc around ch-2 loop, ch 2, 1 FPdc around each of next 3 dc, 1 hdc in 2nd ch at beg of previous row.

Row 26: Ch 1, 1 sc in hdc, ch 2, 1 FPdc around each of next 3 dc, (ch 2, 1 bo dc around each of the next 6 dc) across, ending with 1 FPdc around each of next 3 dc, ch 2, 1 sc in 2nd ch at beg of previous row.

Row 27: Work 1 sc in each dc, 2 sc around each ch loop, and 1 sc in each sc.

Row 28: Ch 1 and then work 1 crab st in each sc across.

Lower edge (towards fingertips): Work 1 sc in each dc and 2 sc around each ch loop. Finish with 1 row crab st. Seam the wrist warmers, beginning at the

Pattern

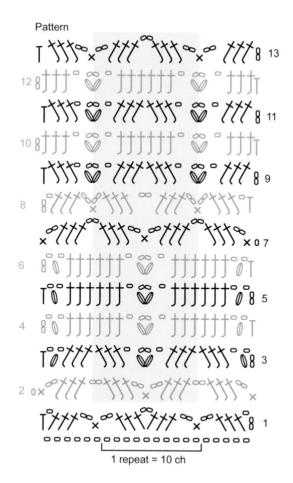

1 repeat = 10 ch

Chart Symbols

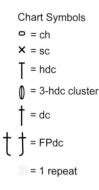

o = ch

✕ = sc

T = hdc

◖ = 3-hdc cluster

† = dc

† † = FPdc

▢ = 1 repeat

finger tips and sewing down about ¾ in / 2 cm; skip 1¼ in / 3 cm for thumbhole and then seam down to bottom edge. Work a round of sc around the thumbhole. Weave in all ends neatly on WS.

Headband, Boot Toppers, and Wrist Warmers

Accessories are quick to make. They're wonderful hostess gifts, or you can set them aside until birthdays or holidays arrive. If you want to use up a little yarn from your stash, you can change colors on every other round—try it! The boot toppers can be folded over the edge of your shoes or pulled up on your legs.

LEVEL OF DIFFICULTY
Intermediate

SIZE
One size

FINISHED MEASUREMENTS
HEADBAND
Circumference: 20½ in / 52 cm
Height: 4 in / 10 cm

MITTENS
Circumference: approx. 7 in / 18 cm

BOOT TOPPERS
Circumference: 11¾ in / 30 cm
Length: 6 in / 15 cm

MATERIALS
Yarn:
CYCA #3 (DK/light worsted), Du Store Alpakka Sterk (40% Merino wool, 40% alpaca, 20% polyamide, 150 yd/137 m / 50 g)

Yarn Color and Amounts:
Burgundy 832
Headband: approx. 40 g
Mittens: approx. 70 g
Boot Toppers: approx. 55 g

Crochet Hook: U.S. size G-6 / 4 mm for the headband and boot toppers; U.S. size E-4 / 3.5 mm for the mittens

GAUGE
1 repeat over 8 ch in pattern on larger hook = 1½ in / 4 cm.
Adjust hook size to obtain correct gauge if necessary.

TECHNIQUES
Front post single crochet (FPsc): Insert the hook at the right side of a st, from front to back; push the hook behind the stitch, and to the front again on the left side of the st; catch yarn and bring through. Finish the stitch as for a regular sc.

21

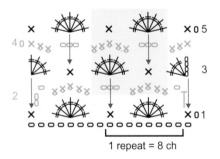

1 repeat = 8 ch

Chart Symbols

‑ = ch

× = sc

✗ = sc in back loop

† = tr

↓ = work tr into sc in direction of arrow

▨ = 1 repeat

PATTERN (MULTIPLE OF 8 + 1 STS)

Row 1: Beg in the 2nd ch from hook, 1 sc, (skip 3 ch, 7 tr in next ch, skip 3 ch, 1 sc in next ch) across.

Row 2: Ch 3 (= 1st hdc + ch 1), skip 1 tr, work (1 front post sc in each of the next 5 tr, ch 3, skip 1 tr + 1 sc + 1 tr) across, ending with 1 FP sc in each of the next 5 tr, ch 1, and 1 hdc in last sc.

Row 3: Ch 4 (= 1st tr), 3 tr in sc of Row 1, skip 2 sc, [1 sc in next sc (the center sc of the 5), 7 tr in the next sc of Row 1, skip 2 sc] across, ending with 1 sc in the next sc (the center sc of the 5), 4 tr in the last sc of Row 1.

Row 4: Ch 1, 1 sc in 1st tr, 1 FP sc in each of the next 2 tr, (ch 3, skip 1 tr + 1 sc + 1 tr, 1 FP sc in each of the

next 5 tr), across, ending with ch 3, skip 1 tr + 1 sc + 1 tr, 1 front post sc in each of the next 2 tr, 1 sc in 4th ch of previous row.

Row 5: Ch 1, 1 sc in 1st sc, [skip 2 sc, 7 tr in next sc 2 rows below, skip 2 sc, 1 sc in next sc (the center of the 5)] across, ending with 1 sc in last sc.
Rep Rows 2-5.

BOOT TOPPERS

Cuff: With hook U.S. size G-6 / 4 mm, ch 49. Work back and forth in pattern until piece measures approx. 2½ in / 6 cm, ending with either Row 2 or 4 in pattern.

Edging:

Row 1: Ch 1, 1 sc around each ch-3 loop and 1 sc in back loop of each sc.

Rows 2-8: Ch 3, 1 dc in each st across.

Cut yarn and re-attach at lower right side with RS facing. Ch 1 and then work 2 sc around each ch loop, 1 sc in sc and 1 sc in ch where the 7 tr were worked.

Row 9: Ch 1 and work 1 crab st in each sc. Sew or crochet to join the piece at center back.

Make the second boot topper the same way. Weave in all ends neatly on WS.

MITTENS

Cuff: With hook U.S. size E-4 / 3.5 mm, ch 41. Work back and forth in pattern until cuff measures approx. 2¾ in / 7 cm, ending with either Row 2 or 4 in pattern.

Next Row: Ch 1 and then work 1 sc around each ch-3 loop and 1 sc through back loop of each sc.

Next Row: Ch 1 and then work 1 crab st in each sc. Seam cuff and cut yarn.

Attach yarn at seamline of the foundation chain.

Rnd 1: Ch 1 and then work 2 sc around each ch loop, 1 sc in each sc, and 1 sc in the ch where the 7 tr were worked, ending rnd with 1 sl st into 1st sc = 31 sc.

Rnd 2: Ch 3, 1 dc in each sc, ending with 1 sl st into 3rd ch at beg of rnd.

Rnds 3-4: Ch 3, 1 dc in each dc, ending with 1 sl st into 3rd ch at beg of rnd.

Rnds 5-7, thumb gusset: Ch 3, 2 dc in next dc, 1 dc in each st until 1 dc rem, 2 dc in last dc, 1 sl st into 3rd ch at beg of rnd = 37 dc at end of Rnd 7.

Rnd 8: Work 1 sl st in each of the next 5 dc, ch 3, 1 dc in each dc until 4 dc rem, ch 3, 1 sl st into 3rd ch at beg of rnd. A total of 9 dc have been skipped for the thumbhole.

Rnd 9: Ch 3, 1 dc in each dc, 3 dc around ch-3 loop, ending with 1 sl st into 3rd ch at beg of rnd = 31 dc.

Rnds 10-16: Work as for Rnd 3.

Rnd 17: Ch 3, (2 dc tog over the next 2 dc, 1 dc in next dc) around, ending with 1 sl st into 3rd ch at beg of rnd.

Rnd 18: Ch 3, (2 dc tog over the next 2 dc) around, ending with 1 sl st into 3rd ch at beg of rnd.

Cut yarn, leaving a long end. Gather rem sts with end and tighten; fasten off.

Thumb: Attach yarn on inner side of thumbhole.

Rnd 1: Ch 3 and then work 14 dc around thumbhole, ending with 1 sl st into 3rd ch at beg of rnd.

Rnds 2-4: Ch 3 and then work 1 dc in each of the next 14 dc, ending with 1 sl st into 3rd ch at beg of rnd.

Rnds 5-6: Shape as for Rnds 17-18 at mitten top and finish as for mitten top.

Make the second mitten the same way. Weave in all ends neatly on WS.

HEADBAND

With hook U.S. size G-6 / 4 mm, ch 97. Work back and forth in pattern until piece measures approx. 3½ in / 9 cm, ending with either Row 2 or 4 in pattern.

Edging:

Row 1: Ch 1, 1 sc around each ch-3 loop and 1 sc in back loop of each sc.

Row 2: Ch 1 and then work 1 crab st in each sc across.

Cut yarn and re-attach at lower right side with RS facing. Ch 1 and then work 2 sc in each ch loop, 1 sc in sc, and 1 sc in ch where the 7 tr were worked.

Row 3: Ch 1 and then work 1 crab st in each sc. Seam the headband at center back. Weave in all ends neatly on WS.

Black and Gray Bag

This bag can be crocheted quickly, since it's worked with such a heavy yarn. The black leather straps ramp up the style!

LEVEL OF DIFFICULTY
Intermediate

FINISHED MEASUREMENTS
Circumference: 31½ in / 80 cm
Length: 16½ in / 42 cm

MATERIALS
Yarn:
CYCA #6 (super bulky), Svarta Färet Home Sweet Home (55% cotton, 45% acrylic, 55 yd/50 m / 100 g)

Yarn Colors and Amounts:
Black 01: 300 g
Gray 03: 400 g

Notions: Leather strap set for handbags (Prym article 615186 Debra)

Crochet Hook: U. S. K-10½ or L-11 / 7 mm

GAUGE
Approx. 9 sc = 4 in / 10 cm.
Adjust hook size to obtain correct gauge if necessary.

TECHNIQUES
Double crochet group (dc gr): work 9 dc into the same stitch.
Double crochet cluster (dc cl): work 9 joined dc (work to but not including last step of each dc and then yarn over hook and through all loops on hook).

PATTERN (MULTIPLE OF 8 STS)

Rnd 1: Ch 1, 1 sc in 1st sc, (skip 3 sc, 9 dc in next sc, skip 3 sc, 1 sc in next sc) around, ending with 1 sl st into 1st sc.

Rnd 2: Ch 3 (= 1st dc), skip 1st sc, 4-dc cl over the next 4 dc, [ch 3, 1 sc in next dc (the center of the 9 dc), ch 3, 9-dc cl over the next 4 dc + 1 sc + 4 dc] around, ending with 5-dc cl over the last 4 dc + 1 sc; 1 sl st into 3rd ch at beg of rnd.

Rnd 3: Ch 3, 4 dc in top of the 5-dc cl, (skip 3 ch, 1 sc in sc, skip 3 ch, 9 dc in top of 9-dc cl) around, ending with 4 dc in top of 4-dc cl and then 1 sl st into 3rd ch at beg of rnd.

Rnd 4: Ch 4 (= 1st sc + ch 3), [9-dc cl over the next 4 dc + 1 sc + 4 dc, ch 3, 1 sc in next dc (the center of the 9 dc), ch 3] around, ending with 1 sl st into 1st ch at beg of rnd.

Rnd 5: Ch 1, 1 sc in 1st sc, (skip 3 ch, 9 dc in top of 9-dc cl, skip 3 ch, 1 sc in sc), around, ending with 1 sl st into 1st sc.

Rep Rnds 2-5.

See also chart on page 13.

BASE

With Black, ch 30 and begin in the 2nd ch from the hook.

Rnd 1: Work 2 sc in the 1st ch, 1 sc in each of the next 27 ch, and 3 sc in last ch; turn and, in the opposite side of foundation chain, work 1 sc in each of the next 27 ch and end with 1 sc in the last ch = 60 sc.

Rnd 2: Pm and move it up on every rnd to indicate beginning of rnd. Work 1 sc in the 1st sc, 2 sc in the next sc, 1 sc in each of the next 27 sc, 2 sc in the next sc, 1 sc in the next sc, 2 sc in the next sc, 1 sc in each of the next 27 sc, 2 sc in the next sc = 64 sc.

Rnd 3: Work 1 sc in each of the 1st 2 sc, 2 sc in the next sc, 1 sc in each of the next 27 sc, 2 sc in the next sc, 1 sc in each of the next 3 sc, 2 sc in the next sc, 1 sc in each of the next 27 sc, 2 sc in the next sc, 1 sc in the last sc = 68 sc.

Rnd 4: Work 1 sc in each of the 1st 3 sc, 2 sc in the next sc, 1 sc in each of the next 27 sc, 2 sc in the next sc, 1 sc in each of the next 5 sc, 2 sc in the next sc, 1 sc in each of the next 27 sc, 2 sc in the next sc, 1 sc in each of the last sc = 72 sc.

SIDES

Rnd 5: Work 1 sc through back loop of each sc around.

Rnds 6-11: Work 1 sc in each sc, ending with 1 sl st into 1st sc of previous rnd.

Rnds 12-21: Change to Gray and work 10 rnds in Pattern.

Rnd 22: Change to Black. Work ch 1, 3 sc around each ch-3 loop and 1 sc into each sc around = 72 sc.

Rnds 23-27: Work 1 sc in each sc around, ending with 1 sl st into 1st sc of previous rnd.

FINISHING

Weave in all ends neatly on WS. Gently steam press bag under pressing cloth to block.

Attach the straps about 1¼ in / 3 in from each side.

Beige Top

This easy-to-crochet top is worked with double crochet stitches only. It'll pair equally well with a long necklace and jeans or dress pants.

LEVEL OF DIFFICULTY
Intermediate

SIZES
XS (S, M, L, XL, XXL)

FINISHED MEASUREMENTS
Chest: 34 (37, 39½, 42½, 45¾, 48½) in / 86 (94, 100, 108, 116, 123) cm
Length: 24½ (25¼, 26, 26¾, 27½, 28¼) in / 62 (64, 66, 68, 70, 72) cm

MATERIALS
Yarn:
CYCA #1 (fingering), Sandnes Garn Mandarin Petit (100% cotton, 195 yd/178 m / 50 g)

Yarn Color and Amount:
Beige 4301: 200 (250, 300, 350, 400, 450) g

Crochet Hook: U. S. E-4 / 3.5 mm

GAUGE
16 sts and 11 rows = 4 x 4 in / 10 x 10 cm.
Adjust hook size to obtain correct gauge if necessary.

Chart Symbols

o = ch

† = dc

TIP FOR DECREASING

When decreasing at the beginning of a row, work a slip stitch over each stitch to be decreased. At the end of a row, turn, leaving stitches to be decreased unworked.

PATTERN

Row 1: Ch 3, 1 dc in each ch across.
Row 2: Ch 3, 1 dc between the 1st and 2nd dc and then between each dc across.
Repeat Row 2.

BACK

Ch 69 (75, 81, 87, 93, 99) and then work back and forth in Pattern until the piece measures 17¾ (18¼, 18½, 19, 19¼, 19¾) in / 45 (46, 47, 48, 49, 50) cm.
Armhole shaping: At each side, on every row, decrease 3 sts 1 time, 2 sts 1 time, and 1 st 3 times. Continue in Pattern until piece measures 23¼ (24, 24¾, 25½, 26½, 27¼) in / 59 (61, 63, 65, 67, 69) cm.
Back neck: Work 16 (17, 18, 19, 20, 21) dc; turn. Decrease 1 st at neck edge on every row 2 times and then fasten off. Count in 15 (16, 17, 18, 19, 20) dc on the other side and pm between the next dc. Shape as for right side to correspond.

FRONT

Work as for back until front measures 15¾ (16½, 17¼, 18¼, 19, 19¾) in / 40 (42, 44, 46, 48, 50) cm. Shape V-neck, and, when at same length as back, shape armholes. Read through the rest of this section *before* you begin crocheting.
V-neck: Work 34 (37, 40, 43, 48, 49) dc; turn. Decrease 1 st at neck edge on every row 12 (14, 16, 18, 20, 22) times.
Armhole shaping: At the side, on every row, decrease 3 sts 1 time, 2 sts 1 time, and 1 st 3 times. After all the decreases, 14 (15, 16, 17, 18, 19) dc remain for shoulder. Continue until the front is same total length as for back and fasten off.
Opposite side of front: Skip the center st and attach yarn at the next dc. Shape as for first side to correspond.

FINISHING

Sew or crochet to join the shoulders and sides. Attach yarn at lower edge of one armhole. Ch 1 and then work approx. 2 sc in every dc / 3 ch around, making sure that the stitches are evenly spaced. Edge the opposite armhole the same way.
Attach yarn at one shoulder seam and work in sc around the V-neck and back neck as for armholes.

Flower Vest

You can make this vest in a variety of sizes and lengths depending on the yarn and hook size you choose. I based the sizing on the chest measurements, so measure a garment you have and use that as a guide for this vest. You can also choose from two lengths for each chest size.

LEVEL OF DIFFICULTY
Advanced

SIZES
See measurements

FINISHED MEASUREMENTS
Measurements with Mandarin Petit with hook U.S. size E-4 / 3.5 mm:
Chest: 37¾ (42½) in / 96 (108) cm
Length: 30¾ in / 78 cm with a total of 8 rows of flowers, 35½ in / 90 cm with a total of 9 rows of flowers.

Measurements with Mandarin Medi with hook U.S. size E-4 / 3.5 mm:
Chest: 44 (49¾) in / 112 (126) cm
Length: 44 in / 112 cm with a total of 8 rows of flowers, 49¾ in / 126 cm with a total of 9 rows of flowers.

Measurements with Mandarin Medi with hook U.S. size G-6 / 4 mm:
Chest: 47¼ (53¼) in / 120 (135) cm
Length: 47¼ in / 120 cm with a total of 8 rows of flowers, 53¼ in / 135 cm with a total of 9 rows of flowers.

MATERIALS
Yarn Choices:
CYCA #1 (fingering), Sandnes Garn Mandarin Petit (100% cotton, 195 yd/178 m / 50 g):
Sand 2431: 300 (400) g
CYCA #3 (DK/light worsted), Sandnes Garn Mandarin Medi (100% cotton, 147 yd/134 m / 50 g): Khaki 2431: 400 (550) g

For all sizes/yarns:
CYCA #3 (DK/light worsted), Dale Garn Gullfasan (90% rayon, 10% nylon 136 yd/124 m / 50 g): Yellow 2633: 100 g for all sizes

Crochet Hook: U. S. E-4 or G-6 / 3.5 or 4 mm

GAUGE
1 flower in Mandarin Petit with hook U.S. size E-4 / 3.5 mm = 4¾ in / 12 cm in diameter.
1 flower in Mandarin Medi with hook U.S. size E-4 / 3.5 mm = 5½ in / 14 cm in diameter.
1 flower in Mandarin Medi with hook U.S. size G-6 / 4 mm = 6 in / 15 cm in diameter.
Measure the first flower and if it's larger than the given measurement, change to a smaller hook; if it's smaller than the given measurement, change to a larger hook.

6-PETALED FLOWER

With Yellow, ch 4 and join into a ring with 1 sl st into 1st ch.

Rnd 1: Ch 3 (= 1st dc), work 11 dc around ring; 1 sl st into 3rd ch at beg of rnd. Cut Yellow.

Rnd 2: Change to Sand/Khaki. Ch 1 and work 1 sc in dc, (ch 11; turn, skip 1st ch, 1 sc in next ch 1 hdc in next ch, 1 dc in next ch, 1 tr in each of the next 2 ch, 1 dc in each of the next 2 ch, 1 hdc in next ch, 1 sc in each of the next 2 ch, 1 sl st in next dc of Rnd 1, 1 sc in next dc) 5 times. Ch 11; turn, skip 1st st, 1 sc in next ch, 1 hdc in next ch, 1 dc in next ch, 1 tr in each of the next 2 ch, 1 dc in each of the next 2 dc, 1 hdc in next ch, 1 sc in each of the next 2 ch, 1 sl st in next dc of 1st rnd, join with 1 sl st in 1st sc of round = 6 petals.

Rnd 3: 1 sl st in each of the next 3 sts (to the ch with 1 dc), (1 sc in each of the next 7 sts, 2 sc in sc at tip, 1 sc in each of the next 7 sts down on the other side, skip 7 sts and begin the next petal) 5 times, 1 sc in each of the next 7 sts, 2 sc in sc at tip, 1 sc in each of the next 7 sts down on the other side, join with 1 sl st into 1st sc.

Rnd 4: (1 hdc in each of the next 7 sc, ch 3, 1 hdc in each of the next 7 sc, 2 sc tog over the next 2 sc) 6 times, join with 1 sl st into 1st hdc.

5-PETALED FLOWER

With Yellow, ch 4 and join into a ring with 1 sl st into 1st ch.

Rnd 1 (RS): Ch 3 (= 1st dc), work 9 dc around ring. Cut Yellow.

Row 2 (RS): Attach Sand/Khaki in 3rd ch at beg of previous rnd with 1 sl st. Ch 1 and work 1 sc in dc, (ch 11; turn, skip 1st ch, 1 sc in next ch, 1 hdc in next ch, 1 dc in next ch, 1 tr in each of the next 2 ch, 1 dc in each of the next 2 ch, 1 hdc in next ch, 1 sc in each of the next 2 ch, 1 sl st in next dc of 1st rnd, 1 sc in next dc) 4 times. Ch 11; turn, skip 1st st, 1 sc in next ch, 1 hdc in next ch, 1 dc in next ch, 1 tr in each of the next 2 ch, 1 dc in each of the next 2 ch, 1 hdc in next ch, 1 sc in each of the next 2 ch, 1 sl st in next dc of Rnd 1; turn = 5 petals.

Row 3: 1 sl st in each of the next 2 sts, (1 sc in each of the next 7 sts, 2 sc in sc at tip, 1 sc in each of the next 7 sts down on other side, skip 7 sts and begin the next petal) 4 times. 1 sc in each of the next 7 sts, 2 sc in sc at tip, 1 sc in each of the next 7 sts down on other side, 1 sl st in next st; turn.

Row 4: Skip 1 sc, (1 hdc in each of the next 7 sc, ch 3, 1 hdc in each of the next 7 sc, 2 sc tog over the next 2 sc) 4 times, 1 hdc in each of the next 7 sc, ch 3, 1 hdc in each of the next 7 sc, 1 sl st in next st. Cut yarn.

4-PETALED FLOWER

Row 1 (RS): Ch 3 (=1st dc), 7 dc around ring; turn.

Rows 2-4: Work as for 5-petaled flower but work repeat only 3 times.

3-PETALED FLOWER

Row 1 (RS): Ch 3 (=1st dc), 5 dc around ring; turn.

Rows 2-4: Work as for 5-petaled flower but work repeat only 2 times.

2-PETALED FLOWER

Row 1 (RS): Ch 3 (=1st dc), 3 dc around ring; turn.

Rows 2-4: Work as for 5-petaled flower but work repeat only once.

Joining: Crochet the flowers together on the last rnd. Instead of ch 3 at the tip of each petal, work ch 1, 1 sl st into previous flower and ch 1.

NOTE: Join the flowers in the sequences shown on the schematic for desired size.

NUMBER OF FLOWERS

Chest: 37¾, 44, or 47¼ in / 96, 112, or 120 cm:
6-Petaled Flowers: 54.
5-Petaled Flowers: 6.
4-Petaled Flowers: 10.

NUMBER OF FLOWERS

Chest: 42½, 49¾, or 53¼ in / 108, 126, or 135 cm:
6-Petaled Flowers: 64.
5-Petaled Flowers: 2.
4-Petaled Flowers: 10.
3-Petaled Flowers: 4.
2-Petaled Flowers: 2.

FINISHING

After all the flowers have been crocheted and joined, work a single crochet edging along the front edges and around the armholes.

Front edging: Attach Sand/Khaki yarn at lower right corner of front, ch 1 and then work sc around the entire opening. Make sure that the stitches are spaced evenly. At the back neck, adjust number of stitches so it doesn't become too wide. Work 3 more rows of sc, trying on the garment as you work to see if you need to increase or decrease a few stitches so the piece will be even. Change to Yellow and work 1 row of sc on RS.

Armhole edging: Attach yarn at base of armhole and crochet edging as for front but work in the round.

Joining flowers for chest sizes 37¾, 44, or 47¼ in / 96, 112, or 120 cm:

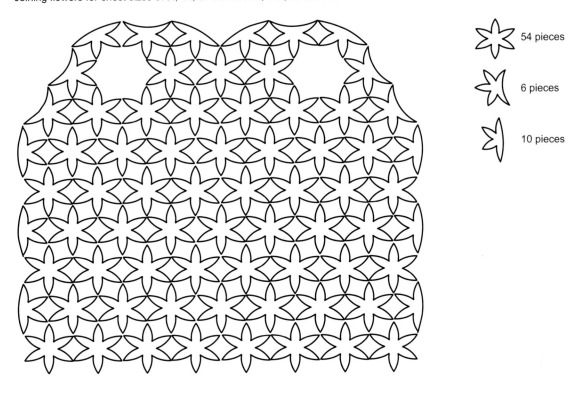

54 pieces

6 pieces

10 pieces

Joining flowers for chest sizes 42½, 49¾, or 53¼ in / 108, 126, or 135 cm:

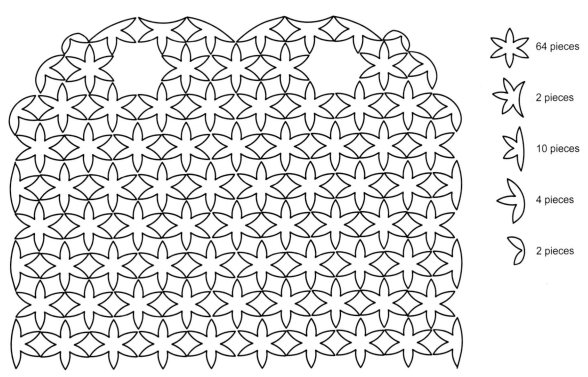

64 pieces

2 pieces

10 pieces

4 pieces

2 pieces

Jacket and Hat in Alpaca Tweed

This jacket features knitted ribbing for the bands and cuffs, while the body and sleeves are crocheted with textured treble stitches. The special stitches give the jacket a lovely structure and the soft tweed yarn simply adds to the effect. To top it off, the raised-stitch fabric is thick and cozy!

LEVEL OF DIFFICULTY
Advanced

SIZES
S (M, L, XL, XXL)

FINISHED MEASUREMENTS
JACKET
Chest: 38½ (41, 43¼, 45¾, 48) in / 98 (104, 110, 116, 122) cm
Length: 30¾ (31½, 32¼, 33, 34) in / 78 (80, 82, 84, 86) cm

HAT
Size: Women's Medium
Circumference: 20½ in / 52 cm

MATERIALS
Yarn:
CYCA #4 (worsted/afghan/Aran), Du Store Alpakka Alpakka Tweed (50% alpaca, 30% Merino wool, 20% synthetic, 87 yd/80 m / 50 g)

Yarn Colors and Amounts:
Light Gray 113: 950 (1050, 1150, 1250, 1300) g for the jacket and 100 g for the hat

Notions: TH Ellesby: 2 buttons art no. 5657-32 for the jacket and 8 buttons for the jacket + 2 for the hat, article no. 5657-40

Crochet Hook: U. S. H-8 / 5 mm

Knitting Needles: U.S. size 8 / 5 mm: long and short circulars

GAUGE
14 sts in crochet pattern = 4 in / 10 cm.
Adjust hook size to obtain correct gauge if necessary.

TECHNIQUES

Ribbed bands and cuffs (knitting):
Row 1: K1 (edge st), k2, (p2, k2) to last st, end k1 (edge st).
Row 2: K1 (edge st), work knit over knit and purl over purl, ending with k1 (edge st).
Rep Row 2.

Front post treble crochet (FPtr):
Wrap yarn twice around the hook. Insert the hook into the right side of the corresponding double crochet stitch 2 rows below (skip the row of single crochet), push the hook around the back of the stitch and then to the front at the left side. Yarn around hook and then complete as a regular treble.

Pattern

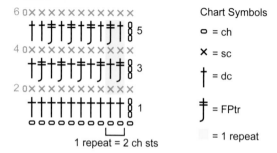

Chart Symbols

o = ch

× = sc

† = dc

‡ = FPtr

▨ = 1 repeat

1 repeat = 2 ch sts

Back post double crochet (BPdc):
Wrap yarn once around the hook. Insert the hook into the right side of the stitch from the wrong side, push the hook to RS, around the stitch, and then out at the left side. Yarn around hook and then complete as a regular double crochet stitch.

PATTERN (MULTIPLE OF 2 + 1 STS)
Row 1: Ch 3 (= 1st dc), 1 dc in each st.
Row 2: Ch 1, 1 sc in each dc.
Row 3: Ch 3 (= 1st dc), (1 FPtr around the corresponding dc 2 rows below, 1 dc in next sc) across.
Row 4: Ch 1, 1 sc in each dc and tr.
Row 5: Ch 3 (= 1st dc), (1 dc in next sc, 1 FPtr around corresponding dc 2 rows below) across, ending with 1 dc each in the last 2 sc.
Rep Rows 2-5.

TIP FOR DECREASING
When decreasing at the beginning of a row, work a slip stitch over each stitch to be decreased. At the end of a row, turn, leaving stitches to be decreased unworked.

TIP FOR INCREASING
Work 2 stitches into the same stitch.

JACKET

BODY
Ribbed lower edge: With knitting needles, CO 172 (180, 184, 192, 200) sts and work back and forth in ribbing for 3¼ in / 8 cm. With RS facing, BO knitwise. Change to crochet and, with RS facing, work 141 (149, 157, 165, 173) BPdc along the ribbing = 1st row of pattern. The stitch loops on the ribbing will now appear as a ridge on the RS. Work back and forth in pattern until piece measures 22½ (22¾, 23¼, 23¾, 24) in / 57 (58, 59, 60, 61) cm. End with a row of FPtr on the RS and then divide the piece at each side for front and back.

LEFT FRONT
Work 32 (34, 36, 38, 40) sc; turn.
Armhole shaping: Continue working back and forth over these stitches. *At the same time*, decrease on every sc row: at armhole edge, decrease 2 sts and then 1 st. After shaping underarm, continue without shaping until armhole depth is approx. 5½ (6, 6¼, 6¾, 7) in / 14 (15, 16, 17, 18) cm.
Neck: On the next row of FPtr, decrease 7 (8, 9, 10, 11) sts at neck edge. Decrease on every row of FPtr 2 sts, then 2 sts, and 1 st = 17 (18, 19, 20, 21) sts rem for the shoulder. After completing final decrease row, cut yarn and fasten off.

RIGHT FRONT
With WS facing, count 31 (33, 35, 37, 39) sts in from the front edge and attach yarn on the next st. Work 32 (34, 36, 38, 40) sc across row. Shape armhole and neck as for left front.

BACK
Begin on WS. Skip 6 sc from the left front and attach yarn in the next st. Work 65 (69, 73, 77, 81) sc; turn. Work back and forth over these sts and, *at the same time*, decrease at each side on every row 2 sts and then 1 st. Continue without shaping until 1 FPtr row less than total length.
Back neck: Work 1 row of FPtr over the outermost 17 (18 19, 20, 21) sts on each side for the shoulders. Join shoulders with slip sts on WS.

SLEEVES

With knitting needles, CO 38 (40, 44, 48, 52) sts and work back and forth in ribbing for 3¼ in / 8 cm. With RS facing, BO knitwise. Change to crochet and, with RS facing, work 33 (37, 41, 45, 49) BPdc along the ribbing = 1st row of pattern. Work back and forth in pattern and, *at the same time*, increase to shape sleeves at each side as follows.

Shaping sleeve: Increase 1 st at each side on the 3rd row of sc. Next, increase 1 st at each side on every other row of sc. Work 1 dc in the increased st on the next row and then work new sts into pattern as quickly as possible. Increase the same way until there are 51 (55, 59, 63, 67) sts total. Now work without shaping until the sleeve is 17¼ (17¾, 18¼, 18½, 18½) in / 44 (45, 46, 47, 47) cm long or to desired length.

Sleeve cap: Decrease 3 sts at the end of each row 6 (6, 7, 7, 8) times and then decrease 5 sts at each side. Cut yarn and fasten off.

POCKETS (MAKE 2 ALIKE)

Ch 21 sts and work back and forth in pattern until piece is approx. 5¼ in / 13 cm long; end with a row of sc. With WS facing, use knitting needle to pick up and knit 24 sts. Make sure that the stitch loops of the sc on RS look smooth and even. Work in ribbing for 1½ in / 4 cm and then BO knitwise. Sew the pockets about 2¾ in / 7 cm up from the ribbing and approx. 2 in / 5 cm in from the band on each front.

FINISHING

Collar: Ch 1 and then work sc evenly along the neck. With knitting needles, pick up and knit 78 (78, 82, 86, 90) sts, making sure that the stitch loops lie toward the RS. Work in ribbing for 7 in / 18 cm and then BO knitwise. Fold the collar in half and sew down neatly on WS.

Left button band: Attach the yarn at the top of the collar, ch 1 and work down evenly in sc. On the collar work sc through both layers and, on the body, work 2 sc over each dc / ch 3 and 1 sc in each sc. Place the last st on the knitting needle and pick up and knit sts with WS facing. Make sure that the stitch loops of the sc lie smoothly on the RS. Work in ribbing until band measures approx. 1½ in / 4 cm. BO on RS knitwise. Pm for the buttons: there are 2 small buttons on the collar and 8 large buttons evenly spaced down the body, approx. 3¼ in / 8 cm apart.

Right buttonhole band: Work as for left band, but make the buttonholes centered over marking for each button on the left band. After working ¾ in / 2 cm, make a buttonhole by binding off 2 sts. On the next row, CO 2 sts over each gap. Continue until right band is same length as left.

Sew or crochet the sleeve seams; attach sleeves.
Weave in all ends neatly on WS.
Gently steam press under a damp pressing cloth.
Sew on buttons.

HAT

With short circular, CO 88 sts. Work back and forth in ribbing for 3¼ in / 8 cm. With RS facing, BO knitwise. Place last st on crochet hook and ch 1. Loosely work 1 sc in each of the 1st 76 sts.

On the next row, work BPdc across (= Row 1 of pattern); this forms a ridge on RS. Continue in pattern, working a total of 10 rows of FPtr and 11 rows sc.

Shape crown: On the next row with FPtr: work FPtr across each dc as before, skipping all the tr = 38 sts rem.

Next row: Work sc2tog across. Cut yarn, thread end through rem sts and tighten. Fasten off.

Sew or crochet the hat at center back. Weave in all ends neatly on WS.

Overlap the short ends of ribbing and sew on 2 buttons (see photo).

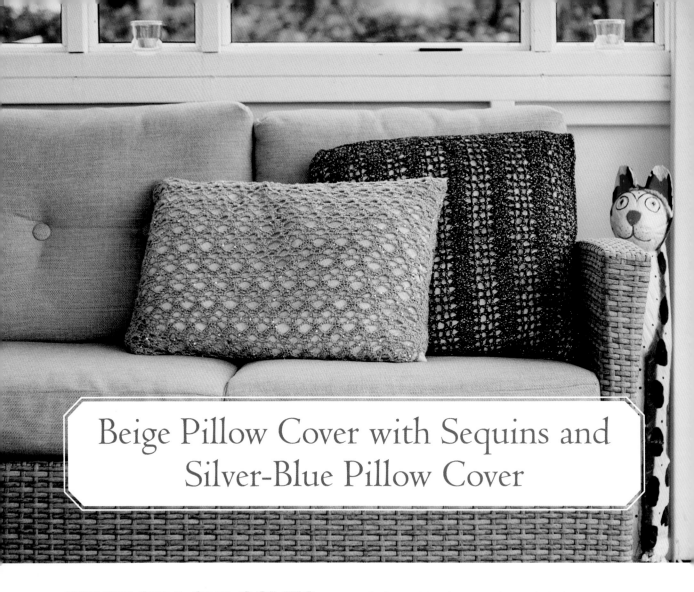

BEIGE PILLOW COVER WITH SEQUINS

LEVEL OF DIFFICULTY
Intermediate

FINISHED MEASUREMENTS
15¾ x 23¾ in / 40 x 60 cm

MATERIALS
Yarn:
CYCA #1 (fingering), Du Store Alpakka Alpakka Wool
(60% alpaca, 40% wool, 182 yd/166 m / 50 g)
CYCA #0 (lace/thread), Du Store Alpakka Bling Effek-
ttråd (100% polyester, 382 yd/349 m / 50 g)

Yarn Colors and Amounts:
Alpakka Wool: Light Beige 505: 200 g
Bling: Beige 3005: 50 g

Notions: Pillow insert, 15¾ x 23¾ in / 40 x 60 cm

Crochet Hook: U. S. E-4 / 3.5 mm

GAUGE
1 rep over 6 ch in Pattern A = approx. 1½ in / 4 cm.
Adjust hook size to obtain correct gauge if necessary.

PATTERN A
See instructions on page 92 and chart below.

Holding one strand of each yarn together, ch 88. Work
back and forth in Pattern A until piece measures 47¼ in
/ 120 cm long. Fasten off.

FINISHING
Gently steam press under a damp pressing cloth. Fold
the piece in half and sew one short side and the long
side. Insert the pillow and seam other short end.

Pattern A

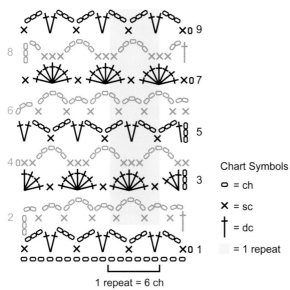

1 repeat = 6 ch

Pattern B

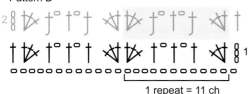

1 repeat = 11 ch

Chart Symbols

o = ch

✕ = sc

† = dc

░ = 1 repeat

SILVER-BLUE PILLOW COVER

LEVEL OF DIFFICULTY
Intermediate

FINISHED MEASUREMENTS
19¾ x 19¾ in / 50 x 50 cm

MATERIALS
Yarn:
CYCA #2 (sport), Rauma Pavo (100% polyester, 170 yd/155 m / 50 g)

Yarn Colors and Amounts:
Blue 2014: 200 g

Notions: Pillow insert, 19¾ x 19¾ in / 50 x 50 cm

Crochet Hook: U. S. K10½ or L-11 / 7 mm

GAUGE
1 rep over 11 ch in Pattern B = approx. 2½ in / 6 cm. Adjust hook size to obtain correct gauge if necessary.

TECHNIQUES
Front post double crochet (FPdc): This stitch is worked as a dc around the post of a dc on the previous row. Wrap yarn once around hook. With RS facing, insert hook from front to back on right side of dc, push hook behind stitch, and then out to the front again on left side of stitch. Yarn around hook and finish dc as usual.
When the WS is facing, insert the hook from back to front, on the right side of the dc, in front of the dc, and out the left side. Yarn around hook and finish dc as usual.

PATTERN B (MULTIPLE OF 11 + 1 STS)
Row 1: Beginning in the 3rd ch from hook, work 3 dc in next ch, [skip 2 ch, work (1 dc in next ch, ch 1, skip 1 ch) 2 times, 1 dc in next ch, skip 2 ch, (3 dc in next ch) 2 times] across, ending with skip 2 ch, (1 dc in next ch, ch 1, skip 1 ch) 2 times, 1 dc in next ch, skip 2 ch, 3 dc in next ch, 1 dc in last st.
Row 2: Ch 3 (=1st dc), (3 dc in next dc, skip 2 dc, 1 FPdc around next dc, ch 1, 1 dc in next dc, ch 1, 1 FPdc around next dc, skip 2 dc, 3 dc in next dc) across, ending with 1 dc in 3rd ch at beg of previous row.
Repeat Row 2.

FRONT
Ch 70 and work back and forth in Pattern B until piece is 19¾ in / 50 cm long. Fasten off.

BACK
Ch 67.
Row 1: Beg in 4th ch from hook, work 1 tr in each ch = 64 tr.
Row 2: Ch 4 (=1st tr), 1 tr in each tr across.
Rep Row 2 until back is 19¾ in / 50 cm long. Cut yarn and fasten off.

FINISHING
Hold the back and front with wrong sides facing each other. Crochet the pieces together from the front with sc along 3 sides; on the 4th side, work sc only into front edge. In each corner, work 3 sc in corner st. Insert pillow form and seam opening.

Pink Cardigan

This cardigan is crocheted with front post double crochet—which means each new stitch is worked around the post of the stitch below, rather than through the top loops. This technique produces a heavier garment than regular double crochet, so this cardigan can be worn as a jacket spring and fall. (This might not be the best design for a beginner, but you can practice with the pillow on page 152, which uses the same pattern stitch!)

LEVEL OF DIFFICULTY
Advanced

SIZES
S (M, L, XL)

FINISHED MEASUREMENTS
Chest: approx. 40¼ (44, 48, 52) in / 102 (112, 122, 132) cm
Length: approx. 30 (30¾, 31¾, 32¼) in / 76 (78, 80, 82) cm
Sleeve length, cuff to underarm: 20½ (20½, 20½, 20½) in / 52 (52, 52, 52) cm

MATERIALS
Yarn:
CYCA #3 (DK/light worsted), Du Store Alpakka Sterk (40% alpaca, 40% Merino wool, 20% nylon, 150 yd/ 137 m / 50 g)

Yarn Colors and Amounts:
Dusty Pink 850: 800 (900, 1000, 1100) g

Notions: 9 buttons from TH Ellesby, art no. 5657-32

Crochet Hook: U. S. G-6 / 4 mm

Knitting Needles: U.S. size 4 / 3.5 mm: set of 5 dpn and short circular

GAUGE
Crochet: 1 rep in Pattern over 10 sts = 2 in / 5 cm.
Knitting: 22 sts in ribbing, lightly stretched = 4 in / 10 cm.
Adjust hook/needle size to obtain correct gauge if necessary.

TECHNIQUES
Front post double crochet (FPdc): This stitch is worked as a dc around the post of a dc on the previous row. Wrap yarn once around hook. With RS facing, insert hook from front to back on right side of dc, push hook behind stitch and then out to the front again on left side of stitch. Yarn around hook and finish dc as usual.

When the WS is facing, insert the hook from back to front, on the right side of the dc, in front of the dc, and out the left side. Yarn around hook and finish dc as usual.

TIP FOR DECREASING
When decreasing at the beginning of a row, work a slip stitch over each stitch to be decreased. At the end of a row, turn, leaving stitches to be decreased unworked.

PATTERN (MULTIPLE OF 10 + 1 STS)
Row 1: Ch 3 (= 1st hdc + ch 1), 1 dc in each of the next 3 ch. [ch 2, skip 2 ch, 1 sc in next ch, ch 2, skip 2 ch, 1 dc in each of the next 2 ch, (1 dc, ch 2, 1 dc) in next ch, 1 dc in each of the next 2 ch] across, ending with ch 2, skip 2 ch, 1 sc in next ch, ch 2, skip 2 ch, 1 dc in each of the next 2 ch (1 dc, ch 1, 1 hdc) in last ch.

Row 2: Ch 1, 1 sc in hdc, ch 2, (1 FPdc around each of the next 3 dc), ch 2, 1 FPdc around each of the next 3 dc, ch 2, 1 sc around ch-2 loop, ch 2) across, ending with 1 FPdc around each of the next 3 dc, ch 2, 1 FPdc around each of the next 3 dc, ch 2, 1 sc in 2nd ch at beg of previous row.

Row 3: Ch 3 (= 1st hdc + ch 1), 3-hdc cl in the 1st sc, ch 1, [1 FPdc around each of the next 6 dc, ch 1, (3-hdc cl, ch 2, 3-hdc cl) in sc, ch 1] across, ending with 1 FPdc around each of the next 6 dc, ch 1, (3-hdc cl, ch 1, 3-hdc cl) in last sc.

Rows 4-6: Ch 3 (= 1st hdc + ch 1), skip 1 ch + 1 hdc-cl, 3 hdc around next ch loop, ch 1, [1 FPdc around each of the next 6 dc, ch 1, (3-hdc cl, ch 2, 3-hdc cl), around next ch-2 loop, ch 1] across, ending with 1 FPdc around each of the next 6 dc, ch 1, 3-hdc cl around next ch, ch 1, 1 hdc in 2nd ch at beg of previous row.

Row 7: Ch 1, 1 sc in hdc, ch 2, (1 FPdc around each of the next 3 dc, ch 2, 1 FPdc around each of the next 3 dc, ch 2, 1 sc around ch-2 loop, ch 2) across, ending with 1 FPdc around each of the next 3 dc, ch 2, 1 FPdc around each of the next 3 dc, ch 2, 1 sc in 2nd ch at beg of previous row.

Row 8: Ch 3 (= 1st hdc + ch 1), (1 FPdc around each of the next 3 dc, ch 2, 1 sc around ch-2 loop, ch 2,

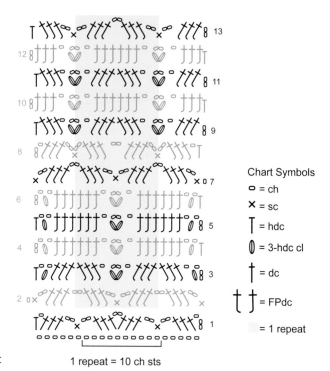

1 repeat = 10 ch sts

Chart Symbols
○ = ch
✕ = sc
⊤ = hdc
◖ = 3-hdc cl
† = dc
†‡ = FPdc
▢ = 1 repeat

1 FPdc around each of the next 3 dc, ch 2) across, ending with 1 FPdc around each of the next 3 dc, ch 2, 1 sc around ch-2 loop, ch 2, 1 FPdc around each of the next 3 dc, ch 1, 1 hdc in last sc.

Row 9: Ch 2 (= 1st hdc), 1 FPdc around each of the next 3 dc, [ch 1, (3-hdc cl, ch 2, 3-hdc cl) in next sc, ch 1, 1 FPdc around each of the next 6 dc] across, ending with ch 1, (3-hdc cl, ch 2, 3-hdc cl) in next sc, ch 1, 1 FPdc around each of the next 3 dc, 1 hdc in 2nd ch at beg of previous row.

Rows 10-12: Ch 2 (= 1st hdc), 1 FPdc around each of the next 3 dc, [ch 1, (3-hdc cl, ch 2, 3-hdc cl) around ch-2 loop, ch 1, 1 FPdc around each of the next 6 dc] across, ending with ch 1, (3-hdc cl, ch 2, 3-hdc cl) in next ch-2 loop, ch 1, 1 FPdc in each of the next 3 dc, 1 hdc in 2nd ch at beg of previous row.

Row 13: Ch 2 (= 1st hdc), (1 FPdc around each of the next 3 dc, ch 2, 1 sc around ch-2 loop, ch 2, 1 FPdc around each of the next 3 dc, ch 2) across, ending with 1 FPdc around each of the next 3 dc, ch 2, 1 sc around ch-2 loop, ch 2, 1 FPdc around each of the next 3 dc, 1 hdc in 2nd ch at beg of previous row.

NOTE: The cardigan is worked in one piece up to the armholes and then divided into front and back. The sleeves are knitted in ribbing as are the button/buttonhole bands and the collar. 1 repeat in pattern is set within brackets [ ], or parentheses ( ), or highlighted with light blue on the chart.

BODY

Ch 202 (221, 241, 261). Work back and forth in pattern for 20 (22, 24, 26) repeats; piece measures 8¼ (8¾, 9, 9½) in / 21 (22, 23, 24) cm long.

Pocket opening: Work 1½ (1½, 2, 2½) rep, ch 20, skip 2 rep, work until 3½ (3½, 4, 4½) rep rem, ch 20, skip 2 rep, and finish row in pattern.

Continue in pattern and pm at each side with 5 (5½, 6, 6½) rep on each front and 10 (11, 12, 13) rep on the back. Work in pattern until piece measures 22¾ (23¼, 23¾, 24) in / 58 (59, 60, 61) cm, ending with a WS row.

RIGHT FRONT

Armhole shaping: Work 4½ (5, 5½, 6) rep on right side and turn. Work only over these repeats until the piece measures 26¾ (27½, 28¼, 29¼) in / 68 (70, 72, 74) cm, ending with a RS row.

Neck shaping: Work 2½ (3, 3½, 4) repeats on WS; turn. On the next row, sl st over the 1st ½ rep and then complete row. Work over the 2 (2½, 3, 3½) rep for the shoulder until the piece measures approx. 30 (30¾, 31¾, 32¼) in / 76 (78, 80, 82) cm. End with the 4th or 10th row of pattern.

LEFT FRONT

Attach yarn ½ rep from side marker on RS. Work as for right front, reversing shaping to match.

BACK

Attach yarn ½ rep from side marker on RS (= total of 1 rep decreased for armholes). Work over the next 9 (10, 11, 12) rep; turn. Continue only over these rep until back is 2 rows less than total length.

Back neck shaping: Work 2 rows over the outermost 2 (2½, 3, 3½) rep for the shoulder at each side.

SLEEVES

With dpn or short circular, CO 64 (68, 72, 76) sts. Join to work in the round and pm for beg of rnd.

Set up ribbing: K1, (p2, k2) to last st and end k1. Work in ribbing for 3¼ in / 8 cm and then increase 1 (with M1) on each side of marker. Increase the same way every 1¼ in / 3 cm 13 times = 90 (94, 98, 102) sts. Continue without shaping until sleeve is 20½ in / 52 cm long or desired length. Bind off in ribbing.

POCKETS

Pocket lining: Pick up and knit approx. 28 sts along the edge of the pocket opening and work back and forth in stockinette with the WS out. On the 1st row, increase 4 sts evenly spaced across = 32 sts. Continue until lining is 7 in / 18 cm long and then bind off. Sew the lining down on WS with small stitches.

Pocket edging: Pick up and knit 24 sts along the lower edge and set up ribbing: k1 (edge st), (k2, p2) 5 times, k2, and k1 (edge st). Work back and forth as est (always knit edge sts) until edging measures 3¼ in / 8 cm and then bind off in ribbing. Fold the edging toward the WS and sew down. Sew the short ends as invisibly as possible to the front.

FINISHING

Sew or crochet the shoulders to join.

Left button band: The front bands are worked separately, folded double and then sewn onto the cardigan after the collar has been knitted. CO 16 sts and set up ribbing: k1 (edge st), (k2, p2) 3 times, k2, k1 (edge st). Continue as est (always knitting edge sts) until the band reaches from the cast-on edge to the neck shaping when slightly stretched. BO the last 7 sts and place rem sts on a holder. Mark spacing for 8 buttons: place the bottom one 1¼ in / 3 cm from lower edge, the top one ¾ in / 2 cm down from the top edge and the rest evenly spaced between. Try to space the buttonholes to align with the pattern. The last button is placed at the center of the collar.

Right buttonhole band: CO 16 sts and set up ribbing: k1 (edge st), (k2, p2) 3 times, k2, k1 (edge st). Continue as est as for left band, but make buttonholes spaced as for buttons. *Buttonhole:* Work 3 sts, BO 2 sts, work 6 sts, BO 2 sts, work 3 sts. On the following row, CO 2 sts over each gap. Work as est until band is same length as for left band. BO the 1st 7 sts and place rem sts on a holder.

Collar: Place 7 sts from the right band on needle, pick up and knit sts evenly spaced along the right front neck, back neck, and along the left front neck, place 7 sts of left band on needle. K1 (edge st), (k2, p2) until 3 sts rem, k2, k1 (edge st). Adjust the stitch count on the 1st row if necessary for ribbing. Work back and forth in ribbing until collar measures 2 in / 5 cm. Make a buttonhole aligned over the previous ones. At 4 in / 10 cm, make another buttonhole. Now continue as est until collar measures 8 in / 20 cm. BO in ribbing. Fold collar in half, making sure that the buttonholes match on each layer. Sew collar down on WS. Fold the button bands lengthwise and sew to front edges. Seam the short ends of the collar. Sew on buttons. At the lower edge of the cardigan, crochet 1 row of sc on RS and then turn and work 1 row of crab stitch (sc worked from left to right).

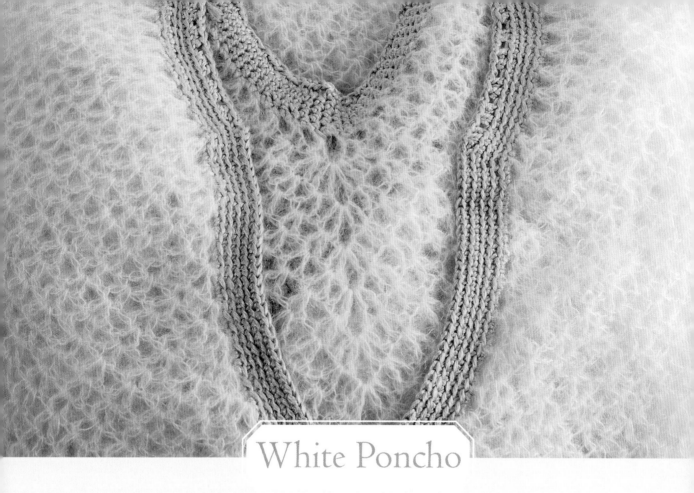

White Poncho

This ethereal poncho is crocheted with a light mohair and silk yarn. To accentuate the beautiful draping, a heavier viscose yarn is used for a border on the lower edge.

LEVEL OF DIFFICULTY
Advanced

SIZES
One size

FINISHED MEASUREMENTS
Length at center front: approx. 41 in / 104 cm

MATERIALS
Yarn:
CYCA #0 (lace), Lang Yarns Mohair Luxe (77% mohair, 23% silk, 191 yd/175 m / 25 g)
Alternate Yarns:
Garnstudio Drops Kid-Silk (75% mohair, 25% silk, 218 yd/199 m / 25 g) or
Sandnes Garn Silk Mohair (60% mohair, 25% silk, 15% wool, 306 yd/280 m / 50 g

CYCA #2 (sport/baby), Garnstudio Cotton Viscose (54% cotton, 46% rayon/viscose, 120 yd/110 m / 50 g)

Yarn Colors and Amounts:
Mohair Lux: White 001: 175 g
Cotton Viscose: Light Beige 17: 200 g

Crochet Hook: U. S. E-4 / 3.5 mm

GAUGE
approx. 7 rep in Pattern over 21 ch and 8 rows = 4 x 4 in / 10 x 10 cm.
Adjust hook size to obtain correct gauge if necessary.

NOTE: Begin by working back and forth to the split at the front and then join to work in the round. Increase on every row/round at center front and center back.

TIP
The poncho is rather long. If you want a shorter garment, you can make adjustments before the 3¼ in / 8 cm wide, beige edging is worked.

and 1 dc around same ch loop. Rep to center back: (1 dc, ch 1, 1 dc) around next ch loop. Around ch-3 loop, work: (1 dc, ch 1, 1 dc, ch 3, 1 dc, ch 1, 1 dc). Rep to center front: (1 dc, ch 1, 1 dc) around next ch loop. Around ch-3 loop, work: (1 dc, ch 1, 1 dc, ch 3, 1 dc, ch 1, 1 dc). Rep to end of rnd: (1 dc, ch 1, 1 dc) around next ch loop. End with 1 sl st in 3rd ch at beg of rnd. Repeat Rnd 13 until piece measures approx. 37¾ in / 96 cm or desired length. Cut Mohair Luxe and fasten off.

Beige edging: Attach Cotton Viscose at ch-3 loop at center back.
Rnd 1: Ch 1, (1 sc, ch 3, 1 sc) around ch-3 loop at center back and center front, with 1 sc in all other sts around. Make sure the stitches don't draw in or ruffle. End rnd with 1 sl st into 1st sc.
Rnds 2-3: Ch 1 and then work 1 sc through back loop on each sc, *except*, at center back and center front, work (1 sc, ch 3, 1 sc) around ch-3 loop; end with 1 sl st into 1st sc.
Rnd 4: Ch 4 and then work 1 dtr through back loop in each sc and (1 dtr, ch 3, 1 dtr) around ch-3 loop at center front and center back. End with 1 sl st into 4th ch at beg of rnd.
Rnd 5: Ch 1 and then work 1 sc through back loop in each dtr and (1 sc, ch 3, 1 sc) around ch-3 loop at center front and center back. End with 1 sl st into 1st sc.
Rnds 6-7: Work as for Rnd 2.
Rnd 8: Work as for Rnd 4.
Rnd 9: Work as for Rnd 5.
Rnds 10-11: Work as for Rnd 2.
Cut yarn and fasten off.

Neckband: Attach Cotton Viscose at one shoulder.
Rnd 1: Ch 1, work 1 sc in each st along neck, 3 sc in corners at neck edge, approx. 3 sc around each dc/ch 3 along each side of the split and 1 sc at base of split; end with 1 sl st in 1st sc. Make sure the edging doesn't draw in or ruffle.
Rnds 2-5: Ch 1, 1 sc through back loop in each sc; in corners, work 3 sc in the center sc of the 3 sc of previous rnd. *At the same time*, decrease at base of split: work sc before the sc at base together with sc in split and next sc = 3 sc tog; end with 1 sl st in 1st sc. Cut yarn and fasten off.

Weave in all ends neatly on WS. Gently steam press poncho under damp pressing cloth.

The Pattern is worked back and forth

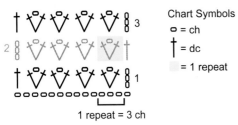

Chart Symbols
o = ch
† = dc
▨ = 1 repeat

1 repeat = 3 ch

With Mohair Luxe, ch 138. Work back and forth in Pattern.
Row 1: Beg in 6th ch from hook (= 1st dc + ch 1), work 1 dc, skip 2 ch, [(1 dc, ch 1, 1 dc) in next ch), skip 2 ch] 21 times. [(1 dc, ch 3, 1 dc) in next ch (= center back, pm in the ch-3 loop), skip 2 ch, [(1 dc, ch 1, 1 dc) in next ch), skip 2 ch] 21 times, (1 dc, ch 1, 1 dc) in next ch.
Row 2: Ch 4 (= 1st dc + ch 1) and 1 dc in 1st dc, work (1 dc, ch 1, 1 dc) in next ch to center back, work (1 dc, ch 1, 1 dc, ch 3, 1 dc, ch 1, 1 dc) in marked ch-3 loop, work (1 dc, ch 1, 1 dc) around next ch across, ending with (1 dc, ch 1, 1 dc) in last dc. Two repeats have been increased at center back and 1 repeat on each side of center front.
Rows 3-12: Work as for Row 2, but end the 12th repeat with ch 3 and 1 sl st into 3rd ch at beg of row.
Rnd 13: 1 sl st around 1st ch, ch 4 (= 1st dc + ch 1)

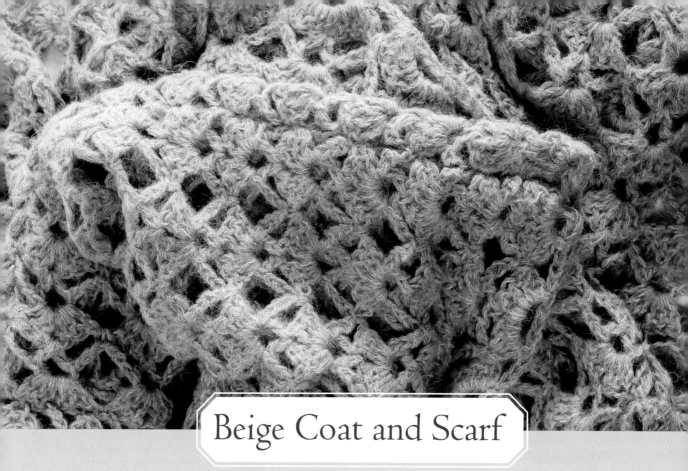

Beige Coat and Scarf

This coat is actually very easy to make! There are no increases or decreases, just rectangles to sew together. The pattern is also easy to memorize, so it's a great beginner project. I made the scarf the same length as the coat, and the outfit looks especially stylish when the scarf hangs straight down. The length of both pieces can easily be adjusted to suit anyone.

COAT
LEVEL OF DIFFICULTY
Easy

SIZES
XS (S, M, L, XL, XXL)

FINISHED MEASUREMENTS
Chest: approx. 35½ (39, 42½, 46, 49¾, 53¼) in / 90 (99, 108, 117, 126, 135) cm; the fronts overlap
Total length: approx. 43¼ (43¼, 43¼, 43¼, 43¼, 43¼) in / 110 (110, 110, 110, 110, 110) cm or desired length
Sleeve length, cuff to underarm: 16¼ (16¼, 17¾, 17¾, 17¾, 17¾) in / 41 (41, 45, 45, 45, 45) cm

SCARF
Approx. 7 x 102 in / 18 x 260 cm

MATERIALS
Yarn:
CYCA #1 (fingering), Rauma Inca (100% alpaca, 191 yd/175 m / 50 g)
+
CYCA #0 (lace), Rauma Alpaca Silk (65% alpaca, 25% silk, 10% Merino wool, 218 yd/199 m / 25 g)

Yarn Colors and Amounts:
Inca: Brown 071: 300 (350, 400, 450, 500, 550) g for the coat and 100 g for the scarf
Alpaca Silk: Beige 1315: 125 (150, 175, 200, 225, 250) g and 50 g for the scarf

Crochet Hook: U. S. J-10 / 6 mm

GAUGE
1 rep over 8 ch and 2 rows in Pattern = approx. 1¾ x 2 in / 4.5 x 5 cm.
Adjust hook size to obtain correct gauge if necessary.

PATTERN (MULTIPLE OF 8 + 1 STS)

Row 1: Beg in 2nd ch from hook, work 1 sc, (ch 5, skip 3 ch, 1 sc in next ch) across.

Row 2: Ch 4 (= 1st tr), work (3 dc, ch 1, 3 dc) around 1st ch-5 loop, [ch 1, skip next ch-5 loop, (3 dc, ch 1, 3 dc) in next ch-5 loop] across, ending with 1 tr in last sc.

Row 3: Ch 1, 1 sc in tr, [ch 3, (1 dc, ch 3, 1 dc) around next ch, ch 3, 1 sc around next ch] across, ending with 1 sc in 4th ch at beg of previous row.

Rep Rows 2-3.

NOTE: For both the coat and scarf, hold 1 strand each Inca and Alpaca Silk together throughout. Each size goes up by one pattern repeat on the back and each front. The fronts overlap slightly at center front, but for some sizes, the stitch count is the same so they won't be too wide.

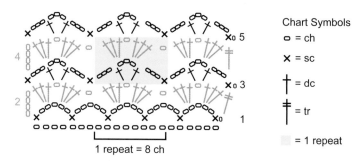

Chart Symbols

o = ch

× = sc

† = dc

‡ = tr

▨ = 1 repeat

1 repeat = 8 ch

COAT

BACK

Holding one strand of each yarn together, ch 82 (90, 98, 106, 114, 122) = 10 (11, 12, 13, 14, 15) repeats. Work back and forth in pattern until back measures 43¼ in / 110 cm (all sizes) or desired length. Cut yarn and fasten off.

RIGHT FRONT

Holding one strand of each yarn together, ch 50 (58, 66, 66, 82, 82) = 6 (7, 8, 8, 9, 9) repeats. Work back and forth in pattern until front measures 43¼ in / 110 cm (all sizes) or same length as back. Cut yarn and fasten off.

LEFT FRONT

Work as for right front.

SLEEVES (MAKE 2 ALIKE)

Holding one strand of each yarn together, ch 50 (58, 66, 66, 82, 82) = 6 (7, 8, 8, 9, 9) repeats. Work back and forth in pattern until sleeve measures 16¼ (16¼, 17¾, 17¾, 17¾, 17¾) in / 41 (41, 45, 45, 45, 45) cm or desired length. Cut yarn and fasten off.

FINISHING

Weave in all ends neatly on WS. Join shoulders until approx. 7 (7½, 8, 8, 8¼, 8¼) in / 18 (19, 20, 20, 21, 21) cm in from each side.

Pin each sleeve with center of sleeve top matching shoulder seam and down each side to same length on each armhole. Sew or crochet sleeves to body and then sew sleeve and side seams.

SCARF

Holding one strand of each yarn together, ch 34. Work back and forth in Pattern until scarf is approx. 102 in / 260 cm long or desired length. Cut yarn and fasten off. Weave in ends neatly on WS.

Fringe: For each fringe, cut 5 strands of each yarn approx. 14 in / 36 cm long. Fold the strands double. Use rug knot to attach the yarn bundles through short ends of scarf, with 4 fringes on each edge.

Striped Jacket

You can crochet either a striped or a blue version of this jacket (see blue jacket on page 58). The tweed yarn chosen for the garment is equally lovely in both the single-color and striped versions. The jacket is longish, shaped at the sides, and has pockets big enough for your keys and cell phone. It will soon be a favorite.

LEVEL OF DIFFICULTY
Advanced

SIZES
XS/S (M, L, XL)

FINISHED MEASUREMENTS
Chest: approx. 37¾ (40½, 43¼, 46) in / 96 (103, 110, 117) cm
Total length: approx. 32¼ (32¾, 33, 33½) in / 82 (83, 84, 85) cm
Width at lower edge: approx. 41¼ (46½, 52, 57½) in / 105 (118, 132, 146) cm
Sleeve length, cuff to underarm: 17¼ (17¾, 18¼, 18½) in / 44 (45, 46, 47) cm

MATERIALS
Yarn:
CYCA #3 (DK/light worsted), Lang Yarns Donegal (100% Merino wool, 208 yd/190 m / 50 g)

Yarn Colors and Amounts:
Blue 25: 150 (150, 200, 200) g
Light Gray 03: 100 (100, 150, 150) g
Gray 05: 100 (100, 150, 150) g
Beige 39: 100 (100, 150, 150) g
Yellow 11: 100 (100, 100, 100) g

Crochet Hook: U. S. G-6 / 4 mm

GAUGE
Approx. 1 rep in Pattern over 9 ch = approx. 1½ in / 3.5 cm.
Adjust hook size to obtain correct gauge if necessary.

Armhole shaping on the left side

Decreasing for the V-neck on the right side of the right front and sleeve

Chart Symbols

⌐ = ch

• = sl st

† = dc

▭ = 1 repeat

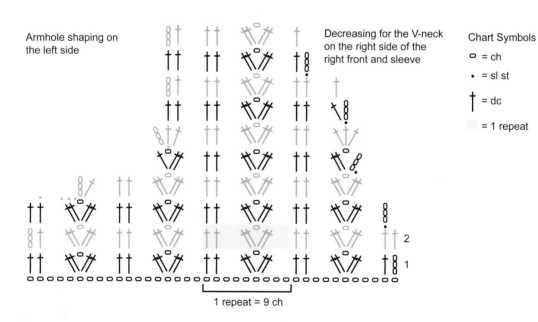

1 repeat = 9 ch

PATTERN (MULTIPLE OF 9 + 2 STS)

Row 1: Ch 3 (= 1st dc), 1 dc in next ch, skip 3 ch, [(2 dc, ch 1, 2 dc) in next ch, skip 3 ch, 1 dc in each of next 2 ch, skip 3 ch] across.

Row 2: Ch 3 (= 1st dc), 1 dc in next ch, [(2 dc, ch 1, 2 dc) around next ch, skip 2 dc, 1 dc in each of the next 2 dc] across. End with 1 dc in 3rd ch of previous row. Repeat Row 2.

STRIPE PATTERN

Work 1 row Blue
Work 1 row Gray
Work 1 row Blue
Work 2 rows Gray
Work 2 rows Yellow
Work 2 rows Beige

Work 4 rows Light Gray
Work 2 rows Blue
Work 2 rows Beige
Work 2 rows Light Gray
Work 2 rows Gray

TIP FOR DECREASING

When decreasing at the beginning of a row, work a slip stitch over each stitch to be decreased. At the end of a row, turn, leaving stitches to be decreased unworked.

TIP FOR INCREASING

Work 2 sts into the same st.

NOTE: If only one stitch count is given, it applies to all sizes.

The striped jacket in the photos is crocheted with Rowan Tweed. This yarn is no longer available, but the Lang Yarns Donegal used for the Blue Jacket can be substituted. The same stripe colors are available in Donegal. The yarn is slightly thinner, though, so the jacket will be slightly smaller than the original.

With first color in stripe sequence or Blue, ch 119 (137, 155, 173). Work back and forth in Pattern = 13 (15, 17, 19) rep across.

Decrease at the sides: Decrease 1 st at each side on every other row 14 times = 9 (11, 13, 15) rep rem. When a ch st is outermost at the side, work it as a dc (see neck shaping on the chart). Work 5 more rows after last decrease row.

Increase at the sides: Now increase 1 st at each side on every other row 7 times = 11 (13, 15, 17) rep. Work the new sts into pattern. Continue until piece measures 23¾ in / 60 cm.

Armhole shaping: At each side on every row, decrease 5-5-1-1 sts (see chart). Work without further shaping until piece measures 32¼ (32¾, 33, 33½) in / 82 (83, 84, 85) cm. Cut yarn and fasten off.

RIGHT FRONT

With first color in stripe sequence or Blue, ch 65 (74, 83, 92). Work back and forth in Pattern = 7 (8, 9, 10) rep across.

Decrease/Increase at the side: Decrease and increase 1 st at the left side as for back. Work until piece measures 19¾ in / 50 cm.

V-neck: Decrease 1 st at the right side on every row 21 times. *At the same time*, when front measures 23¾ in / 60 cm, shape the armhole, at right side, as for back. Continue as est until front is same total length as back. Cut yarn and fasten off.

LEFT FRONT

Work as for right front, reversing shaping to match.

SLEEVES

If you are working the striped jacket, measure 17¼ (17¾, 18¼, 18½) in / 44 (45, 46, 47) cm from the armhole on the body and down. Begin with the stripe in pattern where the measuring tape stops. This ensures that the armhole will begin at the same stripe in the Stripe Pattern of the body.

Ch 56 (65, 74, 83) and work back and forth in Pattern = 6 (7, 8, 9) pattern rep across. Work 5 rows.

Increases: Increase 1 st at each side on every other row 10 times. Continue without further shaping until piece measures 17¼ (17¾, 18¼, 18½) in / 44 (45, 46, 47) cm. Make sure that the stripes for the sleeve and body end at the same place in the Stripe Sequence.

Sleeve cap: At each side, on every row, decrease 5-5-1-1 sts as for back (see chart). Now decrease 1 st at each side 4 (5, 6, 7) times and then 2 sts 4 times.

POCKETS

If you are working the striped jacket, measure approx. 6¼ in / 16 cm up from the lower edge and begin with the stripe the measuring tape hits. Ch 29 (29, 38, 38) and work 12 (12, 13, 13) rows up, ending with 1 row Blue if you are working in stripes.

BELT

With Blue, ch 11 and work in Pattern until piece is approx. 60 (67, 75, 83) in / 150 (170, 190, 210) cm long.

FINISHING

Weave in all ends neatly on WS. Sew or crochet the side, sleeve, and shoulder seams.

Pockets: Sew the pockets securely approx. 1½ in / 4 cm in from the front edge and approx. 6¼ in / 16 cm up from lower edge. If the pockets are striped, make sure the stripes match on pocket and body.

Front bands: Begin at the lower right corner. Work about 3 sc around each dc and 1 sc in each st along back neck. Make sure that the stitch count doesn't cause the edges to ruffle or draw in. The stitch count should be a multiple of 9 + 2 sts. Work back and forth in pattern for 4 in / 10 cm, ending with Blue if working in stripes.

Sew or crochet to attach sleeves.

Belt loops: For each loop, with a doubled strand, ch 8 and attach to side of body at waist.

Blue Jacket

The instructions for this single-color jacket are the same as for the striped version on page 54.

LEVEL OF DIFFICULTY
Advanced

SIZES
XS/S (M, L, XL)

FINISHED MEASUREMENTS
Chest: approx. 37¾ (40½, 43¼, 46) in / 96 (103, 110, 117) cm
Total length: 32¼ (32¾, 33, 33½) in / 82 (83, 84, 85) cm
Width at lower edge: approx. 41¼ (46½, 52, 57½) in / 105 (118, 132, 146) cm
Sleeve length, cuff to underarm: 17¼ (17¾, 18¼, 18½) in / 44 (45, 46, 47) cm

MATERIALS
Yarn:
CYCA #3 (DK/light worsted), Lang Yarns Donegal (100% Merino wool, 208 yd/190 m / 50 g)

Yarn Color and Amount:
Blue 34: 450 (500, 550, 600) g

Crochet Hook: U. S. G-6 / 4 mm

GAUGE
Approx. 1 rep in Pattern over 9 ch = approx. 1½ in / 3.5 cm.
Adjust hook size to obtain correct gauge if necessary.

Long White Scarf with Fringe

A long scarf is always great to have when it's cold out! White is such a delicate color, and it goes with everything. The alpaca and Merino wool yarn I used is very soft and light.

LEVEL OF DIFFICULTY
Intermediate

FINISHED MEASUREMENTS
Width: approx. 11¾ in / 30 cm
Total length: approx. 90½ in / 230 cm + fringe

MATERIALS
Yarn:
CYCA #4 (worsted/afghan/Aran), Lang Yarns Carpe Diem (70% Merino wool, 30% alpaca, 98 yd/90 m / 50 g)
OR

CYCA #4 (worsted/afghan/Aran), Garnstudio Drops Nepal (65% wool, 35% alpaca, 82 yd/75 m / 50 g)

Yarn Color and Amount:
Natural White 94: 400 g

Crochet Hook: U. S. J-10 / 6 mm

GAUGE
1 rep over 14 sts in Pattern = approx. 4 in / 10 cm.
Adjust hook size to obtain correct gauge if necessary.

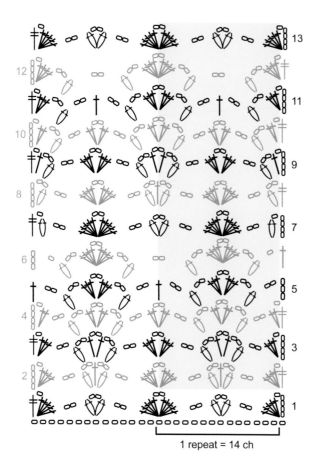

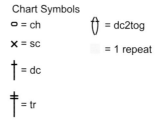

1 repeat = 14 ch

PATTERN (MULTIPLE OF 14 + 1 STS)

Ch 43.

Row 1: Ch 5 (= 1st tr + ch 1), 5 dc in 1st ch, [ch 2, skip 6 ch, (dc2tog, ch 2, dc2tog) in next st, ch 2, skip 6 ch, (5 dc, ch 2, 5 dc) in next ch] across, ending with (5 dc, ch 1, 1 tr) in last st.

Row 2: Ch 5 (= 1st tr + ch 1), 4 dc around 1st ch, [ch 2, skip next ch-2 loop, (dc2tog, ch 2, 1 dc, ch 2, dc2tog) around next ch-2 loop, ch 2, skip next ch-2 loop, (4 dc, ch 2, 4 dc) around next ch-2 loop] across, ending with ch 2, skip next ch-2 loop, (dc2tog, ch 2, 1 dc, ch 2, dc2tog) around next ch-2 loop, ch 2, skip next ch-2 loop, (4 dc, ch 1, 1 tr) in 4th ch at beg of previous row.

Row 3: Ch 5 (= 1st tr + ch 1), 3 dc around 1st ch, [ch 2, skip next ch-2 loop, dc2tog around next ch-2 loop, ch 2, (1 dc, ch 2, 1 dc) in next dc, ch 2, dc2tog around next ch-2 loop, ch 2, skip next ch-2 loop, (3 dc, ch 2, 3 dc) around next ch-2 loop] across, ending with ch 2, skip next ch-2 loop, dc2tog around next ch-2 loop, ch 2, (1 dc, ch 2, 1 dc) in next dc, ch 2, dc2tog around next ch-2 loop, ch 2, skip next ch-2 loop, (3 dc, ch 1, 1 tr) in 4th ch at beg of previous row.

Row 4: Ch 5 (= 1st tr + ch 1), 2 dc around 1st ch, [ch 2,

skip next ch-2 loop, dc2tog around next ch-2 loop, ch 2, (2 dc, ch 2, 2 dc) around next ch-2 loop, ch 2, dc2tog around next ch-2 loop, ch 2, skip next ch-2 loop, (2 dc, ch 2, 2 dc) around next ch-2 loop] across, ending with ch 2, skip next ch-2 loop, dc2tog around next ch-2 loop, ch 2, (2 dc, ch 2, 2 dc) around next ch-2 loop, ch 2, dc2tog around next ch-2 loop, ch 2, skip next ch-2 loop, (2 dc, ch 1, 1 tr) in 4th ch at beg of previous row.

Row 5: Ch 5 (= 1st dc + ch 2), [skip ch-2 loop, dc2tog around next ch-2 loop, ch 2, (3 dc, ch 2, 3 dc) around next ch-2 loop, ch 2, dc2tog around next ch-2 loop, ch 2, skip next ch-2 loop, 1 dc around next ch-2 loop] across, working last dc into the 4th ch at beg of previous row.

Row 6: Ch 4 (= 1st dc + ch 1), skip ch-2 loop, [dc2tog around next ch-2 loop, ch 2, (4 dc, ch 2, 4 dc) around next ch-2 loop, ch 2, dc2tog around next ch-2 loop, ch 2, skip ch-2 loop + 1 dc + ch-2 loop] across, ending with dc2tog around next ch-2 loop, ch 2, (4 dc, ch 2, 4 dc) around next ch-2 loop, ch 2, dc2tog around next ch-2 loop, ch 1 and 1 dc in 3rd ch at beg of previous row.

Row 7: Ch 5 (= 1st tr + ch 1), dc2tog around ch-1 loop, skip ch-2 loop, [(5 dc, ch 2, 5 dc) around next ch-2 loop, ch 2, skip ch-2 loop, (dc2tog, ch 2, dc2tog) around next ch-2 loop, ch 2, skip ch-2 loop] across, ending with (5 dc, ch 2, 5 dc) around next ch-2 loop, ch 2, skip ch-2 loop, dc2tog around ch-1 loop, ch 1, 1 tr in 3rd ch at beg of previous row.

Row 8: Ch 6 (= 1st tr + ch 2), dc2tog around ch-1 loop, ch 2, skip 1st ch-2 loop, [(4 dc, ch 2, 4 dc) around next ch-2 loop, ch 2, skip next ch-2 loop, (dc2tog, ch 2, 1 dc, ch 2, dc2tog) around next ch-2 loop, ch 2, skip next ch-2 loop] across. End with (4 dc, ch 2, 4 dc) around next ch-2 loop, ch 2, skip next ch-2 loop, dc2tog around ch-1 loop, ch 2, 1 tr in 4th ch at beg of previous row.

Row 9: Ch 5 (= 1st tr + ch 1) and 1 dc in tr, ch 2, dc2tog around ch-2 loop, ch 2, skip next ch-2 loop, [(3 dc, ch 2, 3 dc) around next ch-2 loop, ch 2, skip next ch-2 loop, 2 dc-cl around next ch-2 loop, ch 2,

(1 dc, ch 2, 1 dc) in next dc, ch 2, dc2tog around next ch-2 loop, ch 2, skip next ch-2 loop] across, ending with [(3 dc, ch 2, 3 dc) around next ch-2 loop, ch 2, skip next ch-2 loop, dc2tog around next ch-2 loop, ch 2, (1 dc, ch 1, 1 tr) in 4th ch at beg of previous row.

Row 10: Ch 5 (= 1st tr + ch 1), 2 dc cl around ch-1 loop, ch 2, dc2tog around next ch-2 loop, ch 2, skip next ch-2 loop, [(2 dc, ch 2, 2 dc) around next ch-2 loop, ch 2, skip next ch-2 loop, dc2tog around next ch-2 loop, ch 2, (2 dc, ch 2, 2 dc) around next ch-2 loop, ch 2, dc2tog around next ch-2 loop, ch 2, skip next ch-2 loop], ending with (2 dc, ch 2, 2 dc) around next ch-2 loop, ch 2, skip next ch-2 loop, dc2tog around next ch-2 loop, ch 2, (2 dc, ch 1, 1 tr) in 4th ch at beg of previous row.

Row 11: Ch 5 (= 1st tr + ch 1), 3 dc around ch-1 loop, ch 2, dc2tog around ch-2 loop, ch 2, skip next ch-2 loop, [1 dc around next ch-2 loop, ch 2, skip next ch-2 loop, dc2tog around next ch-2 loop, ch 2, (3 dc, ch 2, 3 dc) around next ch-2 loop, ch 2, dc2tog around next ch-2 loop, ch 2, skip next ch-2 loop] across, ending with 1 dc around next ch-2 loop, ch 2, skip next ch-2 loop, dc2tog around next ch-2 loop, ch 2, 3 dc around ch-1 loop, ch 1, 1 tr in 4th ch at beg of previous row.

Row 12: Ch 5 (= 1st tr + ch 1), 4 dc around ch-1 loop, ch 2, [dc2tog around ch-2 loop, ch 2, skip next ch-2 loop + 1 dc + ch-2 loop, dc2tog around next ch-2 loop, ch 2, (4 dc, ch 2, 4 dc) around next ch-2 loop, ch 2] across, ending with dc2tog around ch-2 loop, ch 2, skip ch-2 loop + 1 dc + ch-2 loop, dc2tog around next ch-2 loop, ch 2, 4 dc around ch-1 loop, ch 1, 1 tr in 4th ch at beg of previous row.

Row 13: Ch 5 (= 1st tr + ch 1), 5 dc around ch-1 loop, [ch 2, skip next ch-2 loop, (dc2tog, ch 2, dc2tog) around next ch-2 loop, ch 2, skip next ch-2 loop, (5 dc, ch 2, 5 dc) around next ch-2 loop] across, ending with ch 2, skip next ch-2 loop, (dc2tog, ch 2, dc2tog) around next ch-2 loop, ch 2, skip next ch-2 loop, 5 dc around ch-1 loop, ch 1, 1 tr in 4th ch at beg of previous row.

Rep Rows 2-13 until scarf is approx. 90½ in / 230 cm long or desired length.

Fringe: Cut 8 strands 12¾ in / 32 cm long for each fringe. Fold each bundle in half and attach 7 fringes evenly spaced across each short end of the scarf; tie with rug knot.

White Cardigan

Just the right sweater to pair with your artfully-torn jeans and sun-tanned skin. I crocheted this with a rather thick wool yarn, but it's so lacy and open that it's perfect for northern summers.

LEVEL OF DIFFICULTY
Advanced

SIZES
S/M (L/XL)

FINISHED MEASUREMENTS
Chest: approx. 35½ (51¼) in / 90 (130) cm
Total length: approx. 39½ (39½) in / 100 (100) cm
+ fringe
Sleeve length: 17¾ (17¾) in / 45 (45) cm

MATERIALS
Yarn:
CYCA #4 (worsted/afghan/Aran), Garnstudio Drops
Nepal (65% wool, 35% alpaca, 82 yd/75 m / 50 g)

Yarn Alternative: If you prefer to crochet with a cotton
yarn, try:
CYCA #4 (worsted/afghan/Aran), Garnstudio Paris
(100% Cotton, 82 yd/75 m / 50 g)

Yarn Color and Amount:
Natural White 0100: 800 (950) g

Crochet Hook: U. S. J-10 / 6 mm

GAUGE
1 rep over 14 ch in Pattern A = approx. 4 in / 10 cm.
Adjust hook size to obtain correct gauge if necessary.

dc, ch 2, 3 dc) around next ch-2 loop, 1 dc in 3rd ch at beg of previous row.

Row 3: Ch 3 (= 1st dc), [(3 dc, ch 2, 3 dc) around next ch-2 loop, ch 3, 1 sc around ch-3 loop, 6 dc around ch-5 loop, ch 1] across, ending with (3 dc, ch 2, 3 dc) around next ch-2 loop, 1 dc in 3rd ch at beg of previous row.

Row 4: Ch 3 (= 1st dc), [(3 dc, ch 2, 3 dc) around next ch-2 loop, (ch 1, 1 dc in next dc) 6 times, 1 sc] across, ending with (3 dc, ch 2, 3 dc) around next ch-2 loop, 1 dc in 3rd ch at beg of previous row.

Row 5: Ch 3 (= 1st dc), [(3 dc, ch 2, 3 dc) around next ch-2 loop, ch 3, skip 1 ch + 1 dc + 1 ch + 1 dc, (1 bobble around next ch, ch 2) 3 times, ch 3] across, ending with (3 dc, ch 2, 3 dc) around next ch-2 loop, 1 dc in 3rd ch at beg of previous row.

Row 6: Ch 3 (= 1st dc), skip 3 ch, [(3 dc, ch 2, 3 dc) in next ch-2 loop, ch 5, skip 3 ch + 1 bobble, 1 sc around next ch-2 loop, ch 5, 1 sc around next ch-2 loop, ch 5] across, ending with (3 dc, ch 2, 3 dc) around next ch-2 loop, 1 dc in 3rd ch at beg of previous row.

Row 7: Ch 3 (= 1st dc), [(3 dc, ch 2, 3 dc) in next ch-2 loop, ch 5, skip next ch-5 loop, 1 sc around next ch-5 loop, ch 5] across, ending with (3 dc, ch 2, 3 dc) around next ch-2 loop, 1 dc in 3rd ch at beg of previous row.

Rep Rows 2-7.

TECHNIQUES

Bobble: Work 3 dc around same ch, take hook out of last st loop and insert it into the 1st st of the 3, pick up and draw loop left hanging through loop on hook; tighten.

NOTE: A repeat is set between brackets [ ], or parentheses ( ), or highlighted with light blue on the chart. If only one number is given, it applies to both sizes.

TIP FOR DECREASING

When decreasing at the beginning of a row, work a slip stitch over each stitch to be decreased. At the end of a row, turn, leaving stitches to be decreased unworked.

FRONT AND BACK

Ch 121 (177) and work back and forth in Pattern When piece measures 31½ (30¾) in / 80 (78) cm, or desired length, divide for back and front as follows (the larger size begins the divide earlier because the armhole is wider).

PATTERN (MULTIPLE OF 14 + 9 STS)

Row 1: Ch 3 (= 1st dc), skip 3 ch, [(3 dc, ch 2, 3 dc) in next ch, ch 5, skip 6 ch, 1 sc in next ch, ch 5, skip 6 ch] across, ending with (3 dc, ch 2, 3 dc) in next ch, skip 3 ch, 1 dc in last ch.

Row 2: Ch 3 (= 1st dc), [(3 dc, ch 2, 3 dc) around next ch-2 loop, ch 3, 1 sc around ch-5 loop, ch 5, 1 sc around next ch-5 loop, ch 3] across, ending with (3

Pattern

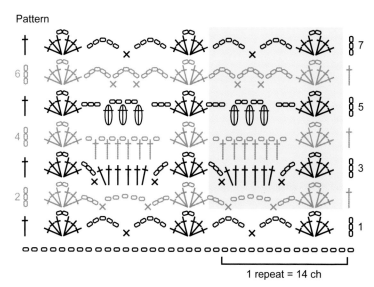

1 repeat = 14 ch

Increasing on the sleeves

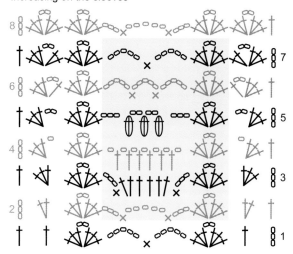

RIGHT FRONT

Crochet over the 1st 2 (3) repeats, ending with (3 dc, ch 2, 4 dc) around ch-2 loop and turn. Begin the next row with ch 3, work (3 dc, ch 2, 3 dc) around ch-2 loop and then work as before, back and forth in Pattern, over these sts until piece measures 37½ in / 95 cm.

Neck: Decrease 1 rep at neck edge and then work without shaping until piece measures 39½ in / 100 cm. Cut yarn and fasten off.

LEFT FRONT

Skip the 4 (6) rep of the back and attach yarn in a ch-2 loop. Work as for right front over the last 2 (3) rep of the row, reversing shaping to match.

BACK

Attach yarn in the same ch-2 loop where the right front ended. Begin with ch 3, (3 dc, ch 2, 3 dc) around the same ch-2 loop and then work over the 4 (6) rep of the back up to the same ch-2 loop where the left front ended. Work (3 dc, ch 2, 4 dc) around same ch-2 loop. On the next row, begin with ch 3, work in pattern as before and end with 1 dc in 3rd ch at beg of previous row. Continue as est until back is same length as front pieces. Cut yarn and end off.

SLEEVES (MAKE 2 ALIKE)

Ch 33 (33) and work back and forth in Pattern. *At the same time,* increase at the sides inside the first/last st. Work 6 (1) rows.

Increasing: Increase 1 dc at each side on every other row 8 (11) times. As they fit in, work the new sts as (3 dc, ch 2, 3 dc) (see chart). Continue as est until sleeve measures approx. 17¾ in / 45 cm.

FINISHING

Sew or crochet shoulder seams.

Attach yarn at neck edge of shoulder seam. Ch 1 and then work 1 rnd of sc evenly spaced around the jacket, ending with 1 sl st into 1st sc; cut yarn and fasten off.

Attach yarn at left neck edge, with WS facing. Ch 1 and then work 1 sc in each sc to the right side of the neck edge; turn and rep the last row.

Cords (make 2 alike): Make a chain cord about 27½ in / 70 cm long; turn. Work 1 sl st into each ch. Cut yarn, leaving a tail so you can attach cord securely to side of neck (see photo).

Fringe: Cut 6 strands, about 8 in / 20 cm long, for each fringe. Make 11 (15) bundles. Attach 1 fringe at the end of each cord and the rest along the lower edge of the cardigan. Attach fringe in the ch st where you crocheted (3 dc, ch 2, 3 dc).

Sweater in Puno Petit Yarn

An openwork sweater with the back slightly longer than the front. It's a perfect sweater for everyday wear!

LEVEL OF DIFFICULTY
Advanced

SIZES
S (M, L, XL, XXL)

FINISHED MEASUREMENTS
Chest: 38½ (42½, 46½, 50½, 54¼) in / 98 (108, 118, 128, 138) cm
Length, front: 22 (22¾, 23¾, 24½, 25¼) in / 56 (58, 60, 62, 64) cm
Length, back: 23¾ (24½, 25¼, 26, 26¾) in / 60 (62, 64, 66, 68) cm
Sleeve length: 17¼ (17¼, 17¼, 17¼, 17¼) in / 44 (44, 44, 44, 44) cm

MATERIALS
Yarn:
CYCA #4 (worsted/afghan/Aran), Rauma Puno Petit (56% alpaca, 34% polyester, 10% Merino wool, 191 yd/175 m / 50 g)
Yarn Color and Amount:
Beige 1314: 300 (350, 400, 450, 500) g

Crochet Hook: U. S. H-8 / 5 mm

GAUGE
1 rep over 8 ch in Pattern A = 2 in / 5 cm.
1 rep over 4 ch in Pattern B = 1 in / 2.5 cm.
Adjust hook size to obtain correct gauge if necessary.

TECHNIQUES
Treble group (tr gr): 4 treble sts worked into same stitch.

PATTERN A (MULTIPLE OF 8 + 1 STS)
Row 1: Ch 1, 1 sc in 1st sc, (ch 2, skip 3 sc, 4 tr in next sc, ch 2, skip 3 sc, 1 sc in next sc) across.
Row 2: Ch 1, 1 sc in 1st sc, (ch 3, 1 sc between the 2 center tr of tr group, ch 3, 1 sc in next sc) across.
Row 3: Ch 4 (= 1st tr), 2 tr in 1st sc, (ch 2, 1 sc in next sc, ch 2, 4 tr in next sc) across, ending with ch 2, 1 sc in next sc, ch 2, 3 tr in last sc.
Row 4: Ch 1, 1 sc in 1st tr, (ch 3, 1 sc in next sc, ch 3, 1 sc between the middle 2 tr in tr group) across, ending with ch 3, 1 sc in next sc, ch 3, 1 sc in 4th ch at beg of previous row.
Row 5: Ch 1, 1 sc in 1st sc, (ch 2, 4 tr in next sc, ch 2, 1 sc in next sc) across.
Rep Rows 2–5.

PATTERN B (MULTIPLE OF 4 + 2 STS)
Row 1 (WS): Beg in 2nd ch from hook, work 1 sc in each ch across.
Row 2: Ch 3 (= 1st dc), (skip 1 sc, 1 dc in each of the next 3 sc, 1 dc in sc you skipped) across, ending with 1 dc in last sc.
Row 3: Ch 1, 1 sc in each dc across.
Rep Rows 2–3.

TIP FOR DECREASING
When decreasing at the beginning of a row, work a slip stitch over each stitch to be decreased. At the end of a row, turn, leaving stitches to be decreased unworked.

TIP FOR INCREASING
Work 2 sts into the same st.

NOTE: A repeat is set between brackets [ ], or parentheses ( ), or highlighted with light blue on the chart.

BACK
Bottom band: Ch 87 (95, 103, 111, 119) and work back and forth in Pattern B for 4¾ in / 12 cm. End with Row 2 of Pattern B = 86 (94, 102, 110, 118) sts. Work Row 3 of Pattern B and increase 1 st at each side and in the center of the piece = 89 (97, 105, 113, 121) sc.
Continue with Pattern A = 11 (12, 13, 14, 15) rep across, until piece measures approx. 22½ (23¼, 24, 24¾, 25½) in / 57 (59, 61, 63, 65) cm. End with Row 2 or 4 of Pattern A.
Back neck: Work 4 (4, 5, 5, 6) rep; turn. Work 1 row over these repeats; cut yarn and fasten off. Attach yarn on opposite shoulder and work to match.

FRONT
Bottom band: Begin as for back but work in Pattern B only until piece measures 3¼ in / 8 cm. Now work in Pattern A until piece measures approx. 20½ (21¼, 22, 22 ¾, 23¾) in / 52 (54, 56, 58, 60) cm, ending with Row 2 of Pattern A.
Neck: Work 4 (4, 5, 5, 6) rep; turn. Work back and forth over these repeats until front is given total length. Work opposite side of neck: skip the next 3 (4, 3, 4, 3) rep, pm, and work opposite side of front to match.

SLEEVES (MAKE 2 ALIKE)
Ch 34 (34, 38, 42, 46) and work back and forth in Pattern B.
Sleeve shaping: Increase 1 dc at each side on every other sc row 10 times. Work new sts into pattern when possible. When sleeve is approx. 17¼ in / 44 cm long, cut yarn and fasten off.

FINISHING
Weave in all ends neatly on WS. Sew or crochet the shoulder seams.
Neckband: Attach yarn at left shoulder. Ch 1 and, in

Pattern A, Body

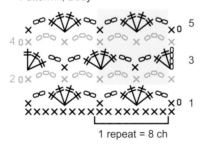

1 repeat = 8 ch

Pattern B, Bands and Sleeves

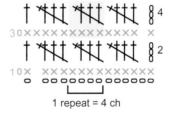

1 repeat = 4 ch

Shaping neck on right side

Chart Symbols

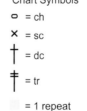

○ = ch

× = sc

† = dc

‡ = tr

░ = 1 repeat

a multiple of 4 sts, sc evenly spaced around neck. Work Rows 2 and 3 of Pattern B and then cut yarn and fasten off.
Pin the center of the sleeve top to the shoulder seam and pin sleeve in place down each side. Make sure the sleeve armhole depths match on each side. Sew or crochet to join sleeves; sew or crochet the side and sleeve seams.

Blue-Violet Pillow Cover

For this lovely pillow cover, I crocheted a rectangle and sewed it over a small ready-made pillow. I like to try out new patterns, especially on a practical project I can use. The yarn for this cover is a heathery sock yarn with silver thread.

LEVEL OF DIFFICULTY
Intermediate

FINISHED MEASUREMENTS
Width: 15¾ in / 40 cm
Length: 11¾ in / 30 cm

MATERIALS
Yarn:
CYCA #1 (fingering), Lang Yarns Mille Colori Socks and Lace Luxe (75% wool, 25% polyamide, 437 yd/400 m / 50 g)

Yarn Colors and Amounts:
Mille Colori: Purple Heather 035: 100 g

Notions: Pillow insert and cover 15¾ x 23¾ in / 40 x 60 cm

Crochet Hook: U. S. E-4 / 3.5 mm

GAUGE
1 rep over 12 ch in Pattern = approx. 2½ in / 6 cm. Adjust hook size to obtain correct gauge if necessary.

TECHNIQUES
Front post single crochet (FPsc): Insert the hook from front to back on the right side of a dc, push hook across back of st and out on left side of dc. Yarn over hook and work as for a regular sc.

PATTERN (MULTIPLE OF 12 + 1 STS)
Ch 98.
Row 1: Beg in 2nd ch from hook, work 1 sc in each of the 1st 4 ch, (skip 2 ch, 5 dc in next ch, skip 2 ch, 1 sc in each of next 7 ch) 7 times, skip 2 ch, 5 dc in next ch, skip 2 ch, 1 sc in each of the last 4 ch.
Row 2: Ch 1, 1 sc in each of the 1st 3 sc, (2 dc in each of next 2 dc, 1 dc in next dc, 2 dc in each of next 2 dc, skip 1 sc, 1 sc in each of next 5 sc, skip 1 sc) 7 times, 2 dc in each of next 2 dc, 1 dc in next dc, 2 dc in each of next 2 dc, skip 1 sc, 1 sc in each of the last 3 sc.
Row 3: Ch 1, 1 sc in each of 1st 2 sc, [(1 dc in next dc, 2 dc in next dc) 4 times, 1 dc in next dc, skip 1 sc, 1 sc in each of next 3 sc, skip 1 sc] 7 times, (1 dc in next dc, 2 dc in next dc) 4 times, 1 dc in next dc, skip 1 sc, 1 sc in each of the last 2 sc.
Row 4: Ch 1, 1 sc in 1st sc, (skip 1 sc, 1 FPsc around each of the next 13 dc, skip 1 sc, 1 sc in next sc) 8 times.
Row 5: Ch 3 and work 2 dc in 1st sc of Row 1, (skip 3 sc, 1 sc in each of next 7 sc, skip 3 sc, 5 dc in corresponding sc on Row 1) 7 times, skip 3 sc, 1 sc in each of next 7 sc, skip 3 sc, 3 dc in last sc of row 1.
Row 6: Ch 2, 2 dc in each of the next 2 dc, (skip 1 sc, 1 sc in each of next 5 sc, skip 1 sc, 2 dc in each of next 2 dc, 1 dc in next dc, 2 dc in each of next 2 dc) 7 times, skip 1 sc, 1 sc in each of next 5 sc, skip 1 sc, 2 dc in each of next 2 dc, 1 dc in 3rd ch at beg of previous row.
Row 7: Ch 3, 1 dc in 1st dc, 2 dc in each of next 2 dc, 1 dc in next dc, [skip 1 sc, 1 sc in each of next 3 sc, skip 1 sc, (1 dc in next dc, 2 dc in next dc) 4 times, 1 dc in next dc] 7 times, skip 1 sc, 1 sc in each of next 3 sc, skip 1 sc, (1 dc in next dc, 2 dc in next dc) 2 times, 1 dc in 3rd ch at beg of previous row.
Row 8: Ch 1, 1 sc in 1st dc, 1 FPsc around each of next 6 dc, (skip 1 sc, 1 sc in next sc, skip 1 sc, 1 FPsc around each of next 13 dc) 7 times, skip 1 sc, 1 sc in next sc, skip 1 sc, 1 FPsc around each of the next 6 dc, 1 sc in 3rd ch at beg of previous row.
Row 9: Ch 1, 1 sc in each of 1st 4 sc (skip 3 sc, 5 dc in corresponding sc on Row 5, skip 3 sc, 1 sc in each of next 7 sc) 7 times, skip 3 sc, 5 dc in corresponding sc on Row 5, skip 3 sc, 1 sc in each of next 3 sc, 1 sc in last sc.

Rep Rows 2-9 until piece measures approx. 11½ in / 29 cm; do *not* cut yarn.
Ch 1 and work 1 rnd sc evenly spaced around the edges, with 3 sc in each corner st.
Sew the crocheted piece to the front of the pillow.

Block Motif Cardigan

Crocheted garments can often become too dense when worked with several colors, but that's not the case here! This Chanel-inspired cardigan is crocheted with a very light and dreamy yarn.

LEVEL OF DIFFICULTY
Advanced

SIZES
S (M, L, XL, XXL)

FINISHED MEASUREMENTS
Chest: 37 (39½, 41¾, 43¾, 46) in / 94 (100, 106, 111, 117) cm
Length: 21¾ (22, 22½, 22¾, 23¼) in / 55 (56, 57, 58, 59) cm
Sleeve length, cuff to underarm: 18¼ (18¼, 18¼, 18¼, 18¼) in / 46 (46, 46, 46, 46) cm

MATERIALS
Yarn:
CYCA #2 (sport/baby), Lang Yarns Nova (48% Merino wool, 32% camel, 20% polyamide, 197 yd/180 m / 50 g)

(CYCA #4 (worsted/afghan/Aran), Lang Yarns Malou Light (72% alpaca, 16% polyamide, 12% wool, 208 yd/190 m / 50 g)

Yarn Colors and Amounts:
Nova:
White 022: 25 (25, 50, 50, 50) g
Light Gray 003: 50 (50, 75, 75, 75) g
Medium Gray 005: 25 (50, 50, 50, 50) g
Charcoal 070: 25 (25, 25, 50, 50) g
Black 004: 50 (50, 50, 50, 50) g
Malou Light:
Yellow 013: 50 g or leftovers for all sizes

Crochet Hook: U. S. G-6 / 4 mm

GAUGE
21 dc and 11 rows of dc = 4 x 4 in / 10 x 10 cm.
Adjust hook size to obtain correct gauge if necessary.

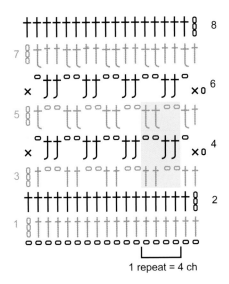

Chart Symbols

o = ch

× = sc

† = dc

†† = raised dc in dc 2 rows below

▨ = 1 repeat

TECHNIQUES

When working 1 dc into a dc 2 rows below, work it around the ch loop 1 row below and into the top of the dc.

The pattern is a multiple of 4 + 2 sts.

TIP FOR INCREASING

Work 2 sts into the same st.

TIP FOR DECREASING

When decreasing at the beginning of a row, work a slip stitch over each stitch to be decreased. At the end of a row, turn, leaving stitches to be decreased unworked.

NOTE: If you want to lengthen the cardigan, make sure you shape the armholes as for the body and sleeves so the patterns will match when you attach the sleeves.

BODY

With Black, ch 198 (210, 222, 234, 248). The instructions for shaping the armholes follow the descrip-

tion of the Stripe pattern. Read through the entire section before you start crocheting.

Bottom Band

Rows 1-2: Ch 3 (= 1st dc). 1 dc in each st.

Row 3 (as for Row 3 of chart), Black: Ch 3 (= 1st dc), 1 dc in next st, (ch 2, skip 2 dc, 1 dc in each of next 2 dc) across, ending with the last dc in the 3rd ch of previous row.

Row 4 (as for Row 4 of chart), White: Ch 1, 1 sc in 1st dc, ch 1, skip 1 dc, (1 dc in each of the next 2 dc of Row 2) across, ending with (ch 1 and 1 sc) in 3rd ch at beg of previous row.

Row 5 (as for Row 5 of chart), Black: Ch 3 (= 1st dc), 1 dc in next dc 2 rows below, (ch 2, skip 2 dc, 1 dc in each of the next 2 dc 2 rows below) across, ending with the last dc in last sc.

Row 6, Light Gray: Work as for Row 4.

Row 7, Black: Work as for Row 5.

Row 8, Yellow: Work as for Row 4.

Row 9, Medium Gray: Work as for Row 5.

Row 10, Light Gray: Work as for Row 4.

Row 11, Black: Work as for Row 5.

Row 12, White: Work as for Row 4.

Row 13 (as for Row 7 of chart), Black: Ch 3, 1 dc in dc 2 rows below, (1 dc in each of the next 2 dc, 1 dc in each of the next 2 dc 2 rows below) across, ending with 1 dc in each of the next 2 dc, 1 dc in next dc 2 rows below, 1 dc in sc.

Rows 14-15, Black: Ch 3 (= 1st dc), 1 dc in each st, ending with last dc in 3rd ch at beg of previous row. Pm at each side with 50 (53, 56, 59, 62) dc on each front and 98 (104, 110, 116, 122) dc on the back. Move markers up as you work.

Stripe Pattern

Rows 16-17, Medium Gray: Work as for Row 14.

Row 18, Light Gray: Work as for Row 14.

Row 19, Light Gray: Work as for Row 3.

Row 20, White: Work as for Row 4.

Row 21, White: Work as for Row 13.

Row 22, Medium Gray: Work as for Row 3.

Row 23, Black: Work as for Row 4.

Row 24, Medium Gray: Work as for Row 5.

Row 25, Black: Work as for Row 4.

NOTE: Rows 23 and 25 are worked with Charcoal on the next repeat of the sequence.

Row 26, Medium Gray: Work as for Row 13.

Rows 27-28, Light Gray:** Work as for Row 14.

(**NOTE:** ** indicates beginning of sleeve patterning.)

Row 29, Light Gray: Work as for Row 3.
Row 30, Medium Gray: Work as for Row 4.
Row 31, White: Work as for Row 5.
Row 32, Medium Gray: Work as for Row 4.
Row 33, Light Gray: Work as for Row 13.
Row 34, Light Gray: Work as for Row 14.
Row 35, Medium Gray: Work as for Row 14.
Row 36, Charcoal: Work as for Row 14.
Row 37, Black: Work as for Row 14.
Row 38, Charcoal: Work as for Row 14.
Rep Rows 16-36 once.
Row 59, Black: Work as for Row 3.
Row 60, Yellow: Work as for Row 4.
Row 61, Black: Work as for Row 5.
Row 62, Charcoal: Ch 3, 1 dc in next dc, (1 dc in each of the next 2 dc 2 rows below, 1 dc in each of the next 2 dc) across, ending with 1 dc in each of the next 2 dc 2 rows below, 1 dc in next dc, 1 dc in 3rd ch at beg of previous row.
Rep from Row 16 and continue in pattern to total length.
NOTE: When at the 33rd row in the Stripe Pattern and piece measures approx. 14½ in / 37 cm for all sizes, divide the piece for back and fronts.

RIGHT FRONT

Armhole shaping: With RS facing, decrease 3-2-1-1 dc at armhole edge on every row as follows. Work 47 (50, 53, 56, 59) dc and turn.
Next Row: Sl st over the next 2 dc and then work to end of row.
Next Row: Work until 1 dc rem; turn.
Next Row: Sl st over next dc and work to end of row = 43 (46, 49, 52, 55) dc. If the stitch count doesn't work evenly into the pattern, work the extra sts in dc. Continue in pattern until piece measures approx. 18½ (19, 19¼, 19¾, 20) in / 47 (48, 49, 50, 51) cm.
Neck shaping: Decrease 7 (9, 11, 13, 15) dc at right side. On every row, decrease 5-3-2-2-1 dc = 23 (24, 25, 26, 27) dc rem. Continue without further shaping until piece measures 21¾ (22, 22½, 22¾, 23¼) in / 55 (56, 57, 58, 59) cm. Cut yarn and fasten off.

LEFT FRONT

With RS facing, count 3 dc after the marker at next side. Attach yarn in the next dc and shape armhole and neck as for right side, reversing shaping to correspond.

BACK

Skip 6 sts from right front (83 sts from side marker) at the next side and attach yarn in next st. Work 92 (98, 104, 110, 116) dc and turn.
Armhole shaping: Shape as for front and then continue in pattern until 2 rows short of total length.
Back neck: Work over the outermost 24 (25, 26, 27, 28) dc for shoulder, decrease 1 st at back neck on the next row. Cut yarn and fasten off. Work the opposite shoulder the same way. Use sl st to seam shoulders with WS facing.

SLEEVES

Ch 46 (50, 54, 58, 62) and work back and forth. Work Rows 1-15 as for lower edge of body.
Sleeve shaping: Work beginning at Row 28 of the Stripe Pattern (marked with **). *At the same time,* increase 1 dc at each side on ever 4th row 13 times = 72 (76, 80, 84, 88) dc. Continue in pattern until sleeve is approx. 18¼ in / 46 cm long. Begin shaping the armhole when at same stripe as on body.
Sleeve cap: Sl st over the 1st 3 dc and work across in pattern until 3 dc rem; turn. Now decrease at each side on every row 2 sts 1 time, 1 st 5 times, 2 sts 3 (4, 5, 6, 7) times, 1 st 10 times, 0 sts 2 times, 1 st 2 times, 2 sts and then 3 sts.

FINISHING

Weave in all ends neatly on WS.
Attach Black yarn at lower edge of left side with WS facing. Work in sc, evenly spaced, up front edge. Work 3 sc in corner at neck shaping and then work evenly in sc along neck. As you work across the back neck, ease in with fewer sts to keep it from becoming too wide. Work 3 sc in the corner and then sc down along the right front; turn. Ch 1 and then work 1 sc in each sc, with 3 sc at each corner (the center st of the previous corner) st by neck. Cut yarn and fasten off. Sew or crochet the sleeve seams and then attach sleeves.

Beige Sweater

This sweater is ready for the party when paired with a skirt or dressy pants. Really, it goes all the way from everyday to festive, so don't hesitate to wear it with jeans!

LEVEL OF DIFFICULTY
Advanced

SIZES
S (M, L, XL)

FINISHED MEASUREMENTS
Chest: 37 (40¼, 43¼, 46½) in / 94 (102, 110, 118) cm
Length: 23¾ (24½, 25¼, 26) in / 60 (62, 64, 66) cm
Sleeve length, cuff to underarm: 18¼ (18½, 19, 19¼ in / 46 (47, 48, 49) cm

MATERIALS
Yarn:
CYCA #0 (lace), Lang Yarns Mohair Luxe (77% Mohair, 23% silk, 191 yd/175 m / 25 g)

(CYCA #2 (sport/baby), Garnstudio Drops Cotton Viscose (54% cotton, 46% rayon, 120 yd/110 m / 50 g) You can substitute Garnstudio Kid Silk or Sandnes Garn Silk Mohair for the Mohair Luxe.

Yarn Colors and Amounts:
Lang Mohair Luxe: Beige 139: 125 (150, 175, 200) g
Cotton Viscose: Light Beige 17: 150 g for all sizes

Crochet Hook: U. S. E-4 / 3.5 mm

GAUGE
Approx. 7 rep in Pattern over 21 ch x 8 rows = 4 x 4 in / 10 x 10 cm.
Adjust hook size to obtain correct gauge if necessary.

Pattern worked back and forth

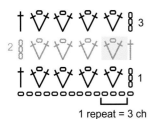

1 repeat = 3 ch

Chart Symbols
- • = sl st
- ○ = ch
- † = dc
- ▨ = 1 repeat

Armhole shaping at right side

PATTERN WORKED BACK AND FORTH (MULTIPLE OF 3 + 2 STS)

Row 1: Beg in 6th ch from hook, work (1 dc, ch 1, 1 dc) in same ch, skip 2 ch, [[1 dc, ch 1, 1 dc) in next ch, skip 2 ch] around until 2 ch rem, skip 1 ch, 1 dc in last ch.

Row 2: Ch 3 (= 1st dc), (1 dc, ch 1, 1 dc) around 1st ch, [[1 dc, ch 1, 1 dc) around next ch] across, ending with 1 dc in 3rd ch of previous row.
Rep Row 2.

PATTERN WORKED IN THE ROUND (MULTIPLE OF 3 STS)

Rnd 1: Ch 4 (= 1st dc + ch 1), and 1 dc in 1st ch, [skip 2 ch, (1 dc, ch 1, 1 dc) around next ch] around, ending with 1 sl st into 3rd ch at beg of rnd.

Rnd 2: 1 sl st around 1st ch, ch 4 (= 1st dc + ch 1) and 1 st around same ch, [[1 dc, ch 1, 1 dc) around next ch] around, ending with 1 sl st into 3rd ch at beg of rnd.
Rep Rnd 2.

TIP FOR DECREASING

When decreasing at the beginning of a row, work a slip stitch over each stitch to be decreased. At the end of a row, turn, leaving stitches to be decreased unworked.

NOTE: A repeat is set between brackets [ ], or parentheses ( ), or highlighted with light blue on the chart.

FRONT

With Mohair Luxe, ch 98 (113, 128, 143). Work back and forth in pattern until piece measures 16½ (17, 17¼, 17¾) in / 42 (43, 44, 45) cm.

Armhole shaping: See also chart. 1 sl st in each of the 1st 8 sts, ch 3 and continue in Pattern as before until 3 rep rem + 1 dc. Work 1 dc around next ch; turn. Sl st in each of the 1st 2 sts, ch 3 and continue in pattern across until 2 rep + 1 dc rem. End with

1 dc around next ch; turn. Rep the last row 2 more times. Continue without further shaping until piece measures 20 (21, 21¾, 22½) in / 51 (53, 55, 57) cm.

Neck: Work in Pattern across the 1st 4 (5, 6, 7) rep + 1 dc around next ch; turn. Work back and forth until piece measures 23¾ (24½, 25¼, 26) in / 60 (62, 64, 66) cm. Cut yarn and fasten off. Now attach yarn at left side and work in Pattern over the outermost 4 (5, 6, 7) rep, ending with 1 dc around next ch. Work until second shoulder is same length as first. Cut yarn and fasten off.

BACK

Begin and work as for front. Shape armholes when at same length. Continue until back is 2 rows less than total length.

Back neck: Shape as for front neck.

SLEEVES (MAKE 2 ALIKE)

With Cotton Viscose, ch 44 (48, 52, 56). Join into a ring with 1 sl st into 1st ch; pm for beg of rnd and move marker up each rnd.

Rnd 1: Ch 1 and then work 1 sc in each ch.

Rnds 2-4: Ch 1 and work 1 sc through both loops of each sc; end with 1 sl st into 1st sc.

Rnd 5: Ch 4 and then work 1 dtr through back loop of each sc, ending with 1 sl st into 4th ch at beg of rnd.

Rnd 6: Ch 1 and work 1 sc through both loops of each dtr. End with 1 sl st into 1st sc.

Rnds 7-8: Ch 1 and work 1 sc through back loop of each sc, ending with 1 sl st into 1st sc.

Rnds 9-12: Work as for Rnds 5-8, but increase 1 sc at each side of marker on the 10th and 12th rnds. Change to Mohair Luxe and work in Pattern for 9 (10, 11, 12) rnds. Change to Cotton Viscose.

Rnd 1: Ch 1 and then work 1 sc in each dc and ch and increase 1 sc on each side of marker = 50 (54, 58, 62) sc.

Rnds 2-12: Ch 1 and work 1 sc through both loops

in each sc. *At the same time*, increase 1 st on each side of marker on the 5th and 10th rnds = 54 (58, 62, 66) sts.

Rnd 13: Ch 4 and then work 1 dtr through back loop of each sc, ending with 1 sl st into 4th ch at beg of rnd.

Rnds 14-16: Ch 1 and then work 1 sc through back loop in each sc. End with 1 sl st into 1st sc. *At the same time*, increase 1 st at each side of marker on Rnd 14.

Rep Rnds 13-16 3 more times. Increase 1 sc on each side of marker on every rep of Rnd 14 = 62 (66, 70, 74) sc.

Next Rnd: Ch 4 and then work 1 dtr through back loop of each sc. End with 1 sl st through 4th ch at beg of rnd

Sleeve cap: Work 1 sl st in each of the next 5 dtr and then ch 1, 1 sc in each dtr until 5 dtr rem before marker; turn.

Read remaining instructions before you continue working.

Work through both loops for remain of work.

Work 5 (7, 9, 9) rows in sc through both loops, 1 row dtr, 3 (3, 3, 5) rows sc, 1 row dtr, 2 rows sc, 1 row dtr, 1 row sc. *At the same time*, decrease at each side on every row: 3 sts 1 time, 2 sts 3 times, 1 st 9 (11, 13, 15) times, and 2 sts 1 time. Cut yarn and fasten off.

FINISHING

Weave in all ends neatly on WS. Sew or crochet the side seams and shoulders.

Braids around the sleeves: Work in sl st around the sleeves with 4 strands of Cotton Viscose (see photo). Hold the strands on the WS where the rnd begins and bring a loop through to the RS, work 1 sl st in every other sc around the sleeve. It is important that you crochet rather loosely. Try on the sleeve to make sure it isn't too tight.

Neckband: Attach one strand of Cotton Viscose at left shoulder seam. Ch 1 and then work in sc evenly spaced around neck; pm at beginning of rnd. Work 1 sc through back loop in every sc for 3 rnds. If the neckline looks too wide, work 2 sc tog spaced out in the 2nd and 3rd rnds. Work a total of 4 rnds in sc and then end with 1 sl st in 1st sc of rnd.

Sew or crochet sleeves to body. Gently steam press under a damp pressing cloth.

Striped Skirt

A fun skirt, crocheted from side to side and closed with a zipper at center back. The possibilities for color combinations are endless—just make sure one stripe is a strong contrast color so the crochet design shows up well.

LEVEL OF DIFFICULTY
Advanced

SIZES
S (M, L, XL)

FINISHED MEASUREMENTS
Circumference at waist: 32¼ (34¾, 37, 39½) in / 82 (88, 94, 100) cm (adjustable)
Circumference at hip: approx. 37 (39½, 41¾, 44) in / 94 (100, 106, 112) cm
Length: 17¾ (17¾, 20, 20) in / 46 (47, 48, 49) cm

MATERIALS
Yarn:
CYCA #2 (sport/baby), Rauma Tumi (50% alpaca 50% wool, 142 yd/130 m / 50 g)

Yarn Colors and Amounts:
Beige SFN 61: 200 (250, 300, 350) g
Rust 0178: 150 (200, 250, 250) g
Yellow 1410: 50 g or small amounts for all sizes

Notions: 2 buttons, 1 beige separating zipper 13¾ (13¾, 15¾, 15¾) in / (35, 35, 40, 40) cm or length to fit

Crochet Hook: U. S. E-4 / 3.5 mm

GAUGE
1 rep in Pattern over 12 ch = 2½ in / 6 cm.
Adjust hook size to obtain correct gauge if necessary.

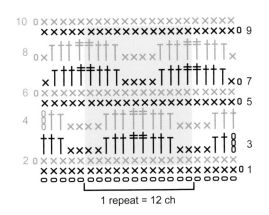

Chart Symbols

○ = ch

✕ = sc

T = hdc

† = dc

‡ = tr

░ 1 repeat

1 repeat = 12 ch

PATTERN (MULTIPLE OF 12 + 10 STS)

Rows 1-2: Ch 1, 1 sc in each st.

Row 3: Ch 3, (1 dc, 1 hdc, 1 sc in each of next 4 sc, 1 hdc, 2 dc, 2 tr, 1 st) across, ending with 1 dc, 1 hdc, 4 sc, 1 hdc, 2 dc.

Row 4: Ch 3, (1 dc, 1 hdc, 1 sc in each of next 4 sc, 1 hdc, 2 dc, 2 tr, 1 dc) across, ending with 1 dc, 1 hdc, 4 sc, 1 hdc, 2 dc.

Rows 5-6: Ch 1 and then work 1 sc in each st across.

Row 7: Ch 1, 1 sc, (1 hdc, 2 dc, 2 tr, 2 dc, 1 hdc, 1 sc in each of the next 4 sc) across, ending with 1 hdc, 2 dc, 2 tr, 2 dc, 1 hdc, 1 sc.

Row 8: Ch 1, 1 sc, (1 hdc, 2 dc, 2 tr, 2 dc, 1 hdc, 1 sc in each of the next 4 sc) across, ending with 1 hdc, 2 dc, 2 tr, 2 dc, 1 hdc, 1 sc.

Rows 9-10: Work as for Rows 5-6.
Rep Rows 3-10.

Circumference: The skirt is calculated for two lengths. If you want a longer skirt, ch 12 more sts and work an extra repeat. That adds about 2½ in / 6 cm.

SKIRT

With Beige, ch 82 (82, 94, 94). Work back and forth in Pattern in the following stripe sequence:

5 rows Beige
(4 rows Rust, 4 rows Beige) 3 times
4 rows Rust
3 rows Beige
(2 rows Rust, 2 rows Beige) 4 (5, 6, 7) times
2 rows Rust
3 rows Beige
(4 rows Rust, 4 rows Beige) 5 times
4 rows Yellow
(4 rows Beige, 4 rows Rust) 2 times
3 rows Beige
(2 rows Rust, 2 rows Beige) 4 (5, 6, 7) times
2 rows Rust
3 rows Beige
(4 rows Rust, 4 rows Beige) 4 times
1 row Beige

WAISTBAND

Try on the skirt occasionally as you work to make sure the waist fits. If you want it a bit smaller, decrease a few more stitches evenly spaced across each row.

Row 1: Attach yarn with 1 sl st at top corner at right. Work 1 row sc evenly spaced along the top edge. Make sure it fits well. At the end of the row, ch 10 for the button band.

Row 2: Ch 3 and work 1 dc in each of the next 11 sc, (dc2tog over the next 2 sc, 1 dc in each of the next 3 sc) across.

Row 3: Ch 3, (1 dc in each of next 7 dc, dc2tog over the next 2 dc) across, but do not decrease over the last 15 dc.

Rows 4-6: Ch 3 and work 1 dc in each dc across.

Row 7 (RS): Ch 1 and work 1 sc in each dc across.

FINISHING

Work 1 row crab st along each side of center back. Work 1 row sc along the lower edge.
Sew in zipper and sew 2 buttons on the right side of the waistband. Use the space between 2 dc as the buttonholes.

Light Blue Dress

You can wear this dress with a solid-color slip underneath, or throw it over a bikini or swimsuit. It is crocheted in flattering A-line shaping with a lovely cotton/linen yarn.

LEVEL OF DIFFICULTY
Advanced

SIZES
S (M, L, XL)

FINISHED MEASUREMENTS
Chest: 30 (34¼, 37¾, 41¾) in / 76 (86, 96, 106) cm
Circumference, bottom hem: 51¼ (55¼, 59, 63) in / 130 (140, 150, 160) cm
Total length: approx. 33½ (35½, 35½, 37½) in / 85 (90, 90, 95) cm, including 1½ in / 4 cm edging
Sleeve length to underarm: 4 (4, 4, 4 in / 10 (10, 10, 10) cm, including 1½ in / 4 cm edging

MATERIALS
Yarn:
CYCA #4 (worsted/afghan/Aran), Sandnes Garn Line (53% cotton, 33% other, 14% linen, 120 yd/110 m / 50 g)

Yarn Color and Amounts:
Light Blue 2005: 550 (600, 650, 700) g

Crochet Hook: U. S. G-6 / 4 mm

GAUGE
16 tr and 5 rows in pattern = 4 x 4 in / 10 x 10 cm
Adjust hook size to obtain correct gauge if necessary.

Pattern

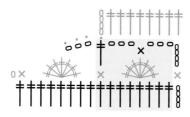

4

20

3

1

1 repeat = 8 cm

Chart Symbols

o = ch

X = sc

† = tr

█ 1 repeat

Neck shaping on right side

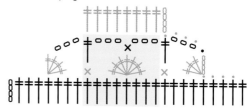

0

Armhole shaping

PATTERN (MULTIPLE OF 8 + 1 STS)
Row 1: Ch 4, 1 tr in each st across.
Row 2: Ch 1, 1 sc in 1st tr, (skip 3 tr, 7 tr in next tr, skip 3 tr, 1 sc in next tr) across, ending with last sc in 4th ch at beg of previous row.
Row 3: Ch 7 (= 1st tr + ch 3), [skip 3 tr, 1 sc in next tr (the center tr of the 7), ch 3, 1 tr in next sc, ch 3] across, ending with 1 sc in the center tr of the 7, ch 3, 1 tr in last sc.
Row 4: Ch 4, (3 tr around ch-3 loop, 1 tr in sc, 3 tr around next ch-3 loop, 1 tr in tr) across, ending with last tr in 4th ch at beg of previous row.
Rep Rows 2-4.

TIP FOR DECREASING
When decreasing at the beginning of a row, work a slip stitch over each stitch to be decreased. At the end of a row, turn, leaving stitches to be decreased unworked. If decreasing in the middle of a row, work 2 tr tog.

NOTE: A repeat is set between brackets [ ], or parentheses ( ), or highlighted with light blue on the chart. On size S, 1 rep less is worked in length, and on size XL 1 rep more is worked than on sizes M and L. This is adjusted at the lower edge before the shaping begins.

BACK
Work back and forth in Pattern while, at the same time, shaping on the treble crochet rows.

Ch 113 (121, 129, 137). Work 3 (6, 6, 9) rows. On the next row (= Row 4 of pattern), decrease 8 tr evenly spaced across. Work 6 rows and then decrease 8 tr evenly spaced across the next row (= Row 4 of pattern). Decrease the same way every 7th row (= every other time you work Row 4 of pattern), a total of 6 times = 65 (73, 81, 89) tr / 8 (9, 10, 11) rep. Continue without further shaping until piece measures approx. 22¾ (24½, 24½, 26) in / 58 (62, 62, 66) cm and the last row is Row 4 of pattern.
Armhole shaping: Decrease as shown on the chart on the next 2 rows and then work without further shaping until armhole depth is approx. 7 (7, 8, 8) in / 18 (18, 20, 20) cm. End on Row 3 (3, 4, 4) of pattern.
Back neck: Work in tr over the 2 outermost repeats for all sizes = 17 tr. Cut yarn and reattach so you can work the last 2 outermost repeats on the opposite side.

FRONT
Begin and work as for the back until piece measures approx. 24 (25½, 25½, 27¼) in / 61 (65, 65, 69) cm. End with Row 4 of pattern.
Neck shaping: Work 3 repeats (for all sizes) and then decrease as shown on the chart. 1 rep is eliminated and 2 rep rem for shoulder. Continue on the rem rep until front is same total length as back. Work the opposite side the same way.

SLEEVES

Ch 49 (57, 57, 65). Work back and forth in Pattern for 4 rows.

Armhole, Row 5: 1 sl st in each of the 1st 4 tr, ch 4 and work 3 tr in the same tr as last sl st, (skip 3 tr, 1 sc in next tr, skip 3 tr, 7 tr in next tr) 4 (5, 5, 6) times, skip 3 tr, 1 sc in next tr, skip 3 tr, 4 tr in next tr.

Row 6: Ch 3, [1 tr in next sc, ch 3, skip 3 tr, 1 sc in next tr (the center tr of the 7), ch 3] 4 (5, 5, 6) times, 1 tr in next sc, ch 3, 1 sl st into 4th ch at beg of previous row.

Row 7: 3 sl st around ch-3 loop and 1 sl st in 1st tr, ch 4, (3 tr around ch-3 loop, 1 tr in sc, 3 tr around next ch-3 loop, 1 tr in tr) across.

Row 8: Ch 1, 1 sc in 1st tr, (skip 3 tr, 7 tr in next tr, skip 3 tr, 1 sc in next tr) across.

Row 9: 1 sl st in each of next 3 tr, [1 sc in next tr (the center tr of the 7), ch 3, 1 tr in next sc, ch 3, skip 3 tr] across, ending with 1 sc in the center tr of the last tr group.

Row 10: Ch 4, (3 tr around ch-3 loop, 1 tr in sc, 3 tr around ch-3 loop, 1 tr in tr) across, ending with 3 tr around last ch-3 loop and 1 tr in sc.

Rep Rows 8-10 one time and then rep Rows 8-9; end size S here.

Sizes M, L, and XL only:

Row 16: 1 sl st in each of next 3 ch and next tr, ch 4, 3 tr around ch-3 loop, 1 tr in sc, 3 tr around next ch-3 loop, 1 tr in tr.

Sizes L and XL only:

Row 17: 1 sl st in each of next 2 tr, ch 4, 1 tr in each tr until 2 tr rem. Cut yarn and fasten off.

FINISHING

Weave in all ends neatly on WS. Sew or crochet shoulder, side, and sleeve seams.

Neckband: Begin on right shoulder, ch 1 and then work in sc around neck with approx. 4 sc around each tr / ch 4 loop, ending with 1 sl st into 1st sc.

Edging at lower edge (multiple of 8 sts):

Rnd 1: Attach yarn at a side seam. Ch 1 and then work 1 sc in each st, ending with 1 sl st into 1st sc.

Rnd 2: Ch 1, 1 sc in each of next 4 sc, (1 sc, ch 7, 1 sc) in next sc, 1 sc in each of next 7 sc) around, ending with (1 sc, ch 7, 1 sc) in next sc, 1 sc in each of the last 3 sc, end with 1 sl st into 1st sc.

Rnd 3: Ch 3 (= 1st dc), 1 sc in next sc, (9 sc around ch-7 loop, skip 2 sc, 1 sc in next sc, 1 dc in next sc, 1 sc in next sc) around, ending with 9 sc around ch-7

loop, skip 2 sc, 1 sc in next sc, 1 sl st into 3rd ch at beg of rnd.

Rnd 4: Ch 1, 1 sc in 3rd ch of previous rnd, [ch 4, skip 4 sc that were worked around ch-7 loop, (1 sc, ch 5, 1 sc) in next sc (the center sc of the 9), ch 4, 1 sc in next dc] around, ending with 1 sl st into 1st sc.

Rnd 5: Ch 1, 1 sc in sc, (3 sc around ch-4 loop, 4 sc around ch-5 loop, 3 sc around ch-4 loop, 1 sc in sc) around, ending with 1 sl st into 1st sc.

Sleeve edging: Attach yarn at seam and work as for edging around lower edge of dress.

Sew or crochet to join sleeves to body.

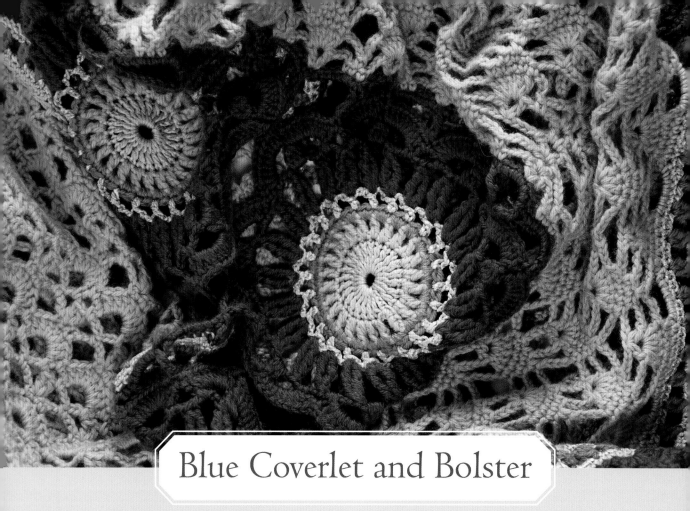

Blue Coverlet and Bolster

A coverlet and bolster in refreshing blue tones. If you don't feel up to starting with the large coverlet, try the bolster first instead.

LEVEL OF DIFFICULTY
Advanced

FINISHED MEASUREMENTS
Coverlet: approx. 47¼ x 67 in / 120 x 170 cm
Bolster: 19¾ in / 50 cm long and 21¼ in / 54 cm in circumference

MATERIALS
Yarn:
CYCA #2 (sport/baby), Dale Garn Falk (100% wool, 116 yd/106 m / 50 g).
CYCA #2 (sport/baby), Garnstudio Cotton Viscose (54% cotton, 46% rayon/viscose, 120 yd/110 m / 50 g).
CYCA #3 (DK/light worsted), Dale Garn Gullfasan (90% rayon, 10% nylon, 136 yd/124 m / 50 g).

Yarn Colors and Amounts:
Falk:
Light Blue 5822: 500 g for the coverlet; 50 g for bolster
Denim Blue 5744: 350 g for the coverlet; 100 g for bolster
China Blue 5943: 50 g for the coverlet; 50 g for bolster
Gullfasan: Silver 4911: 100 g for the coverlet and 50 g for bolster
Cotton Viscose: Light Beige 17: 100 g for the coverlet and 50 g for bolster

Notions: Insert pillow 19¾ x 6¾ in / 50 x 17 cm in diameter for the bolster

Crochet Hook: U. S. G-6 / 4 mm

GAUGE
A circle is 8 in / 20 cm in diameter.
Adjust hook size to obtain correct gauge if necessary.

Patterns A

Pattern A

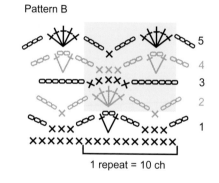

Pattern B

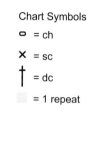

Chart Symbols

○ = ch

✕ = sc

† = dc

▨ = 1 repeat

1 repeat = 10 ch

1 repeat = 6 ch

TECHNIQUES

Treble cluster (tr cl): Work each tr except last step and end with yarn over hook and through all loops on hook.

Double crochet cluster (dc cl): Work each dc except last step and end with yarn over hook and through all loops on hook.

Picot: Ch 3, 1 sl st into 1st ch.

PATTERN A (MULTIPLE OF 6 + 1 STS)

Row 1: Beg in 2nd ch from hook, work 1 sc, (ch 3, skip 2 ch, 2 dc in same st, ch 3, skip 2 sts, 1 sc in next st) across.

Row 2: Ch 5 (= 1st dc + ch 2), 1 sc around 1st ch-3 loop, (ch 3, 1 sc around ch-3 loop, ch 5, 1 sc around next ch-3 loop) across, ending with ch 3, 1 sc around next ch-3 loop, ch 2, 1 dc in last sc.

Row 3: Ch 3, and 3 dc in dc, (1 sc around ch-3 loop, 7 dc around ch-5 loop) across, ending with 1 sc around ch-3 loop and 4 dc in 3rd ch at beg of previous row.

Row 4: Ch 1, 1 sc in each of the 1st 2 dc, [ch 5, skip 2 dc + 1 sc + 2 dc, 1 sc in each of the next 3 dc (the center sts of the 7)] across, ending with ch 5 and 1 sc in last dc and 1 sc in 3rd ch at beg of previous row.

Row 5: Ch 3 and 1 dc in sc, [ch 3, 1 sc around ch-5 loop, ch 3, skip 1 sc, 2 dc in next sc (the center of the 3)] across, ending with ch 3, 1 sc around ch-5 loop, ch 3, 2 dc in last sc.

Row 6: Ch 3, 1 sc around 1st ch-3 loop, (ch 5, 1 sc around next ch-3 loop, ch 3, 1 sc around next ch-3 loop) across, ending with ch 5, 1 sc around next ch-3 loop, ch 2, 1 sc in 3rd ch at beg of previous row.

Row 7: Ch 1, 1 sc in sc, (7 dc around ch-5 loop, 1 sc around next ch-3 loop) across, ending with 7 dc around ch-5 loop, 1 sc in ch at beg of previous row.

Row 8: Ch 5 (= 1st dc + ch 2), skip 2 dc, (1 sc in each of the next 3 dc, ch 5, skip 2 dc + 1 sc, + 2 dc) across, ending with 1 sc in each of the next 3 dc, ch 2, 1 sc in last sc.

Row 9: Ch 1, 1 sc in dc, (ch 3, skip 1 sc, 2 dc in same sc, ch 3, 1 sc around ch-5 loop) across, ending with ch 3, skip 1 sc, 2 dc in same sc, ch 3, 1 sc in 3rd ch at beg of previous row.

Rep Rows 2-9.

CIRCLE

With Beige, ch 8. Join into a ring with 1 sl st into 1st ch.

Rnd 1: Ch 4 (= 1st tr), 23 tr around ring.

Rnd 2, Light Blue: Ch 4 (= 1st dc + ch 1), (1 dc in next tr, ch 1) 23 times total, end with 1 sl st into 3rd ch at beg of rnd.

Rnd 3, China Blue: Ch 1, 2 sc around each ch around, end with 1 sl st into 1st sc.

Rnd 4, Silver: Ch 5 (= 1st dc + ch 2), (skip 1 dc, 1 dc in next dc, ch 2) 23 times total, 1 sl st into 3rd ch at beg of rnd.

Rnd 5, Denim: Ch 5 and 1 tr tr in 3rd ch at beg of previous rnd, ch 4, skip ch-2 loop, (2 tr cl in next dc, ch 4, skip ch-2 loop) 23 times, end with 1 sl st into 5th ch.

Rnd 6: Sl st to center of ch-4 loop, ch 1, (1 sc around ch-4 loop, ch 5, 3-dc cl around next ch-4 loop, ch 5, 1 sc around next ch-4 loop, ch 5) 8 times, 1 sl st into 1st sc.

Rnd 7: 1 sl st to ch-5 loop, ch 3 (= 1st dc), 8 dc around ch-5 loop, ch 3, 9 dc around next ch-5 loop, 1 sc around next ch-5 loop, (9 dc around next ch-5 loop, ch 3, 9 dc around next ch-5 loop), 1 sc around next ch-5 loop) 7 times, 1 sl st into 3rd ch at beg of rnd.

Rnd 7, joining: 1 sl st in ch-5 loop, (9 dc around ch-5 loop, ch 3, 9 dc around next ch-5 loop, 1 sc around next ch-5 loop) 6 times; (9 dc around ch-5 loop, ch 1, 1 sc in previous circle in corresponding ch-3 loop, ch 1, 9 dc around next ch-5 loop, 1 sc around next ch-5 loop) 2 times, 1 sl st into 1st dc.

NARROW PANEL (MULTIPLE OF 3 STS)

Rnd 1, Beige: Ch 1, 1 sc in each st and 3 sc in each corner (the center sc of the 3 sts is the corner st), ending with 1 sl st into 1st sc. For the bolster, omit corners.

Rnd 2, Silver: Ch 1 and then work 1 sc in each st and 3 sc in each corner st, ending with 1 sl st into 1st sc.

Rnd 3, China Blue: Beg in a corner of the coverlet, [(2-dc cl, ch 2, 2-dc cl) in corner, (ch 2, skip 2 sc, 2-dc cl in same st)] until 2 sc before corner st, ch 2, skip 2 sc) around, ending with 1 sl st into 1st dc cl.

Rnd 4, Silver: Ch 1, work 3 sc around each ch-2 loop and 5 sc around each ch-2 loop at each corner; end with 1 sl st into 1st sc.

Rnd 5, Beige: Ch 1 and then work 1 sc in each sc and 3 sc in each corner st, 1 sl st into 1st sc.

EDGING (MULTIPLE OF 13 STS)

Rnd 1, Denim: Attach yarn at a corner, work [(1 sc, ch 3, 1 sc) in corner st, 1 sc in each of the next 10 sc, ch 3, skip 2 sc, (1 sc in each of the next 11 sc, ch 3, skip 2 sc) to next corner st], ending with 1 sl st into 1st dc cl.

Rnd 2: 1 sl st around ch-3 loop, [(2-dc cl, ch 2, 2-dc cl, ch 2, 2-dc cl) around ch-3 loop, ch 2, skip 2 sc, 1 sc in next st, (ch 3, skip 2 sc, 1 sc in next sc) 2 times, ch 2] around, ending with 1 sl st into 1st dc-cl.

Rnd 3: Ch 1 in 1st dc cl, (3 sc around ch-2 loop, 1 picot, 1 sc in next dc cl, 3 sc around next ch-2 loop, 1 picot, 1 sc in next dc cl, 1 sc around ch-2 loop, 2 sc around ch-3 loop, ch 3, 2 sc around next ch-3 loop,

1 sc around ch-2 loop, 1 picot, 1 sc in next dc cl) around, ending with 1 sl st into 1st sc.

BLUE COVERLET

NOTE: Begin by working the center section back and forth and then crochet a narrow border around the entire rectangle. Next, crochet the circles together as explained in pattern. The center section and the circles are sewn together. Crochet around the entire coverlet and end with a narrow border and an edging. When you crochet entirely around the coverlet, adjust the stitch count on the 1st rnd of a new pattern to make sure count is correct for new pattern. Skip an extra st or omit a stitch so the repeat comes out correctly.

CENTER SECTION

With Light Blue, ch 151. Work back and forth in Pattern A until piece measures 15 in / 38 cm. Work a Narrow Panel all around the piece. Along the short sides, work approx. 3 sc around each dc and 1 sc in every sc. Make sure the sts are evenly spaced and the edge doesn't draw in or ruffle.

Circles: Make a total of 16 circles. Crochet them together with a total of 6 circles on each long side and a total of 4 circles on each short side. Make sure you correctly crochet the circles together (see photo, page 93).

Frame around the inside of the circles: Beg on one long side with RS facing you. Beg crocheting on the second circle from the right. Attach the yarn in the 1st free ch-3 loop. Ch 1, [1 sc around ch loop, ch 7, 1 dc in sc, ch 7, 1 sc around next ch-3 loop, ch 7, 1 tr in next sc, ch 7, 1 dtr around sc in the connection between 2 circles, ch 7, 1 tr in sc on next circle, ch 7) rep 3 times; 1 sc around ch loop, ch 7, 1 dc in sc, ch 7, 1 sc around next ch-3 loop, ch 7, 1 tr in next sc, ch 7, 1 tr

tr around sc in connection between 2 circles but do not draw yarn through the last 2 sts on hook, 1 dtr in sc on next circle (corner) do not draw yarn through the last 3 sts on hook, 1 dtr around sc in connection between 2 circles, draw last yo through the last 4 sts on hook (= 3 dtr together, ch 7, 1 tr in sc on next circle, ch 7)]; rep until you've worked around all the circles, EXCEPT on the short sides, where you should work the repeat within square brackets only once. End with 1 sl st in 1st sc. Now work 6 sc around each ch-7 loop and 1 sc in each sc/dc/tr/dtr cl, 1 sl st into 1st sc.

Frame around the outside of the circles: With RS facing, begin on a long side. Begin on the 1st circle from the right. Attach yarn on the 1st ch-3 loop pointing towards you. Work [(1 sc around ch-3 loop, ch 7, 1 dc in sc, ch 7, 1 sc around next ch-3 loop, ch 7, 1 tr in next sc, ch 7, 1 dtr around sc in join between 2 circles, ch 7, 1 tr in sc on next circle, ch 7) 5 times; 1 sc around ch-3 loop, ch 7, 1 dc in sc, ch 7, 1 sc around next ch-3 loop, ch 7, (1 dtr, ch 7, 1 dtr) in next sc (= corner), ch 7] until you've worked around all the circles, EXCEPT on the short sides, where you should work the repeat within square brackets only 3 times. End with 1 sl st into 1st sc.

Now work 6 sc in each ch-7 loop, 7 sc in corner loops, and 1 sc in each sc/dc/tr/dtr, ending with 1 sl st into 1st sc.

Sew or crochet the center section to the circles and then, with Light Blue, work around the entire coverlet in Pattern B. Work ch 3 instead of the 1st dc on each rnd and end with 1 sl st into 3rd ch at beg of rnd. Attach yarn on the center st of a corner.

Rnd 1: Work **(1 dc, ch 3, 1 dc) in corner st, ch 3, skip 1 sc, *1 sc in each of next 3 sc, ch 3, skip 3 sc, (1 dc, ch 2, 1 dc) in same sc, ch 3, skip 3 sc*; rep * to * to next corner st but end with 1 sc in each of the next 3 sc, ch 3**; rep ** to ** 4 times and end with 1 sl st into 1st dc.

Rnd 2: Sl st around ch-3 loop, **(1 dc, ch 3, 1 dc) around ch-3 loop, *ch 4, 1 sc in center sc of the 3, ch 4, 5 dc around ch-2 loop*; rep * to * to next corner, end with ch 4, 1 sc in center sc of the 3, ch 4**; rep ** to ** 4 times and end with 1 sl st into 1st dc.

Rnd 3: Sl st around ch-3 loop, **(1 dc, ch 3, 1 dc) around ch-3 loop, *ch 7, 1 sc in each of next 5 dc*; rep * to * to next corner, end with ch 7**; rep ** to ** 4 times, ending with 1 sl st into 1st dc.

Rnd 4: Sl st around ch-3 loop, **(1 dc, ch 3, 1 dc) around ch-3 loop, ch 3, *skip 3 ch, (1 dc, ch 2, 1 dc) in next ch, ch 3, skip 3 ch, 1 sc in each of next 3 sc, ch 3*; rep * to * to next corner, end by skipping 3 ch, 1 dc, ch 2, 1 dc) in next ch, ch 3**; rep ** to ** 4 times, ending with 1 sl st into 1st dc.

Rnd 5: Sl st around ch-3 loop, **(1 dc, ch 3, 1 dc) around ch-3 loop, ch 4, 1 sc around ch-3 loop, *ch 4, 5 dc around ch-2 loop, ch 4, skip 1 sc, 1 sc in center sc*; rep * to * to next corner, ending with ch 4, 5 dc around ch-2 loop, ch 4**; rep ** to ** 4 times, ending with 1 sl st into 1st dc.

Rep Rnds 3–5 until the pattern is approx. 6¼ in / 16 cm. Work a Narrow Panel and the Edging around the entire coverlet. Weave in all ends neatly on WS. Gently steam press blanket.

BOLSTER

SQUARES

Work Rnds 1–7 as for Circles of coverlet and the continue with Denim:

Rnd 8: Ch 10 (= 1st dc + 7 ch), 1 sc around next ch-3 loop, ch 7, (1 dtr, ch 7, 1 dtr) in next sc, ch 7, 1 sc around next ch-3 loop, ch 7, [1 dc, ch 7, 1 sc around next ch-3 loop, ch 7, (1 dtr, ch 7, 1 dtr) in next sc, ch 7, 1 sc around next ch-3 loop, ch 7] 3 times, and end with 1 sl st into 3rd ch at beg of rnd.

Rnd 9: Ch 1, [1 sc in dc, 6 sc around ch-7 loop, 1 sc in sc, 6 sc around ch-7 loop, 1 sc in dtr, (3 sc, ch 3, 3 sc) around next ch-7 loop, 1 sc in dtr, 6 sc around ch-7 loop, 1 sc in sc, 6 sc around ch-7 loop] 4 times, and end with 1 sl st into 1st sc.

Make 4 squares total and sew them together in pairs. Attach yarn in right corner of a rectangle of 2 squares. Ch 3 and then work 1 dc in each sc along one long side. Rep on the other rectangle and then sew or crochet to join both long sides into a tube. Work the Narrow Panel around each short side.

CIRCLES ON THE SIDES

Work Rnds 1–5 as for the Circles and then continue with Denim:

Rnd 6: Ch 1, (1 sc in dtr-cl, 3 sc around ch-4 loop) around and end with 1 sl st into 1st sc.

FINISHING

Sew or crochet one circle to the side; insert pillow form and then attach the other circle at the opposite end.

Blue Sweater Edged with Green and Headband

This is an easy pattern to follow. I designed this to be a short sweater—so buy one or two extra skeins if you want to lengthen it! It's also fun to try other color combinations, but be sure to choose a color that contrasts well with the main color for the best effect. The headband can also serve as a nice hairband in the summer, if you make it with cotton yarn.

LEVEL OF DIFFICULTY
Intermediate

SIZES
S (M, L, XL)

FINISHED MEASUREMENTS
Chest: 39½ (43¼, 47¼, 51¼) in / 100 (110, 120, 130) cm
Total length: 21¼ (23¼, 23¼, 25¼) in / 54 (59, 59, 64) cm
Sleeve, cuff to underarm: 16½ (16½, 16½, 16½) in / 42 (42, 42, 42) cm
Headband, circumference: 20½ in / 52 cm

MATERIALS
Yarn:
CYCA #4 (worsted/afghan/Aran), Dale Garn Cotinga (70% wool, 30% alpaca, 87 yd/80 m / 50 g).
CYCA #0 (lace), Rowan Kid Silk Haze (70% mohair, 30% silk, 229 yd/209 m / 25 g).

CYCA #3 (DK/light worsted), Sandnes Garn Alpakka (100% alpaca, 120 yd/110 m / 50 g).
Alternate Yarns: Nepal from Garnstudio can be used instead of Cotinga and Kid Silk Haze can be substituted with Kid Silk from Garnstudio or Silk Mohair from Sandes Garn.

Yarn Colors and Amounts:
Sweater:
Cotinga: Blue 5853: 550 (600, 650, 700) g
Kid Silk Haze: Green 597: 50 (50, 50, 50) g
Sandnes Alpakka: Yellow-Green 2005: 100 (100, 100, 100) g
Headband: leftover yarns from the sweater

Crochet Hook: U. S. H-8 / 5 mm

GAUGE
16 tr and 5 rows in Pattern B = 4 x 4 in / 10 x 10 cm.
Adjust hook size to obtain correct gauge if necessary.

SWEATER

PATTERN A (MULTIPLE OF 2 + 1 STS)
Row 1: Ch 1, 1 sc, (ch 1, skip 1 ch, 1 sc in next st) across, ending with 1 sc in last ch.
Row 2: Ch 1, 1 sc in 1st sc, (ch 1, skip 1 sc, 1 sc around next ch) across, ending with 1 sc in last sc.
Rep Row 2.

PATTERN B (MULTIPLE OF 8 + 1 STS)
Row 1: Ch 4, 1 tr in every st across.
Row 2: Ch 1, 1 sc in 1st tr, (skip 3 tr, 7 tr in next tr, skip 3 tr, 1 sc in next tr) across, working last sc into 4th ch at beg of previous row.
Row 3: Ch 7 (= 1st tr + ch 3), skip 3 tr, [1 sc in next tr (the center tr of the 7), ch 3, 1 tr in next sc, ch 3] across, ending with 1 sc in next tr (the center tr of the 7), ch 3, 1 tr in last sc.
Row 4: Ch 4, (3 tr around ch-3 loop, 1 tr in sc, 3 tr around next ch-3 loop, 1 tr in tr) across but work last tr in 4th ch at beg of previous row.
Rep Rows 2-4.

TIP FOR INCREASING
Work 2 stitches into the same stitch.

NOTE: A repeat is set between brackets [ ], or parentheses ( ), or highlighted with light blue on the chart.

BACK
Holding 1 strand each of Kid Silk Haze and Alpakka together, ch 91 (99, 107, 115). Work back and forth in Pattern A until piece measures 3¼ in / 8 cm. Work 1 row of 1 sc in each sc and around each ch and, *at the same time*, skip 10 sts evenly spaced across = 81 (89, 97, 105) fm.
Change to Cortinga and continue in Pattern B, working the 1st row with tr around sc with RS facing: Yarn 2 times around hook, insert hook from back to front in right side of sc. Yarn over hook and complete tr. The stitch loops now form an edge between the edge and body. Work until piece measures approx. 20½ (22½, 22½, 24½) in / 52 (57, 57, 62) cm; end on Row 3 of pattern.
Back neck: Ch 4 (= 1st tr), work 24 (28, 32, 36) tr. Cut yarn and fasten off. Count in from the side and work the opposite shoulder to match.

FRONT
Work as for back until piece measures approx. 19 (21, 21, 22¾) in / 48 (53, 53, 58) cm; end with Row 4 of pattern.
Neck: Work 3 (3½, 4, 4½) rep of Pattern B and then decrease for your size as shown on the chart. Continue until front is same total length as back.

SLEEVES
Holding 1 strand each of Kid Silk Haze and Alpakka together, ch 38 (46, 46, 54). Work back and forth in Pattern A until piece measures 3¼ in / 8 cm. Work 1 row of 1 sc in each sc and around each ch and, at the same time, skip 5 sts evenly spaced across = 33 (41, 41, 49) sc. Change to Cortinga and continue in Pattern B, but work the 1st row with tr wrapped around sc as for back.
Sleeve shaping: Increase 1 tr at each side on every 3rd and 4th row in Pattern B. Work new sts into pattern as possible or work them as tr.
Continue until piece measures 16½ (16½, 16½, 16½) in / 42 (42, 42, 42) cm or desired length; end with Row 4 of Pattern B. Cut yarn and fasten off.

FINISHING
Weave in all ends neatly on WS. Sew or crochet the shoulder seams. Pin the center of the sleeve top at the shoulder seam and then pin sleeve down each side of armhole. Sew or crochet sleeve top to armhole and then seam sleeves and sides.
Neckband: Attach 1 strand Cotinga at right shoulder. Ch 1 and the work in sc: along back neck, work 3 sc around ch loops and 1 sc in each sc and tr; on the front, sc evenly spaced down to tr, 1 sc in each tr and then evenly up to the beginning of the rnd. Work 1 sc in each sc but do not join rnd with sl st. Work 2 rnds sc and then finish last rnd with 1 sl st in next sc.

HEADBAND

With Cotinga, ch 81 and work back and forth as follows:
Rows 1-4: Pattern B.
Row 5: Change to 1 strand each Alpakka and Kid Silk Haze. Ch 1 and then work 1 sc in each st.
Row 6: Ch 1 and then work 1 sc in each sc. Cut yarn and attach 1 strand each Alpakka and Kid Silk Haze at the foundation chain. Work as for Rows 5-6.
Seam headband at center back.

Pattern B

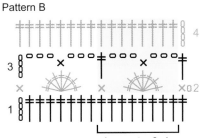

1 repeat = 8 ch

Neck shaping, sizes S and L

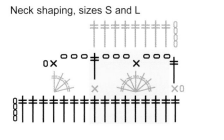

Chart Symbols

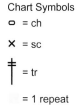

- = ch

✕ = sc

╪ = tr

= 1 repeat

Neck shaping, sizes M and XL

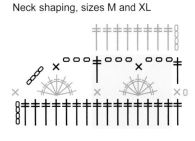

Pattern A

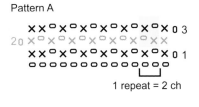

1 repeat = 2 ch

97

Gray Cardigan

A cozy cardigan with bulky yarn and an easy pattern makes for quick crochet! The A-line shaping means it's a great style for anyone. Measure to see what size to make—and remember you can always work it a little large and let the fronts overlap.

LEVEL OF DIFFICULTY
Intermediate

SIZES
XS (S, M/ L, XL, XXL)

FINISHED MEASUREMENTS
Chest: 33 (37¼, 41¾, 46½, 51¼) in / 84 (95, 106, 118, 130) cm
Width at lower edge: approx. 43 (47¼, 51½, 56, 60¼) in / 109 (120, 131, 142, 153) cm
Total length: 34 (34¾, 35½, 36¼, 37) in / 86 (88, 90, 92, 94) cm
Sleeve, cuff to underarm: 19 (19¼, 19¾, 19¾, 20) in / 48 (49, 50, 50, 51) cm
Headband, circumference: 20½ in / 52 cm

MATERIALS
Yarn:
CYCA #6 (super bulky), Garnstudio Drops Andes (65% wool, 35% alpaca, 105 yd/96 m / 100 g).

Yarn Color and Amount:
Dark Gray 0519: 900 (1000, 1100, 1200, 1300) g

Crochet Hook: U. S. M/N-13 / 9 mm

GAUGE
Approx. 8 dc and 6 rows = 4 x 4 in / 10 x 10 cm.
Adjust hook size to obtain correct gauge if necessary.

PATTERN A
Row 1: Ch 3, work 1 dc in each ch across.
Row 2: Ch 3, work 1 dc between the 1st and 2nd dc and then 1 dc between each dc across.
Rep Row 2.

PATTERN B (MULTIPLE OF 3 + 2 STS)
Row 1: Ch 4 (= 1st dc + ch 1), skip 1 ch, 3 dc in next ch, (ch 1, skip 2 ch, 3 dc in next ch) across, ending with ch 1, skip 1 ch, 1 dc in last ch.
Row 2: Ch 3 (= 1st dc), 1 dc around 1st ch, ch 1, (3 dc around next ch, ch 1) across, ending with ch 1, 1 dc around next ch, and 1 dc in 3rd ch at beg of previous row.
Row 3: Ch 4 (= 1st dc + ch 1), 3 dc around 1st ch, (ch 1, 3 dc around next ch) across, ending with ch 1 and 1 dc in 3rd ch at beg of previous rnd.

TIP FOR DECREASING
When decreasing at the beginning of a row, work a slip stitch over each stitch to be decreased. At the end of a row, turn, leaving stitches to be decreased unworked.

TIP FOR INCREASING
Work 2 stitches into the same stitch.

BODY
Ch 71 (80, 89, 98, 107) and then work back and forth in Pattern B for 8 rows.
Next Row: Work 1 dc in each dc, skipping ch sts = 72 (81, 90, 99, 108) dc.
Now, continue working Row 2 of Pattern A. Pm to set off 16 (18, 20, 22, 25) sts for each front and 40 (45, 50, 55, 58) sts for back. Work 2 rows.
Side Shaping: Work dc2tog at each side of each marker = 4 dc decreased on row. Decrease the same way every 3rd row a total of 5 times = 51 (60, 69, 78, 87) dc rem.
Work without further shaping until piece measures 25½ (26, 26½, 26¾, 27¼) in / 65 (66, 67, 68, 69) cm and then begin shaping armholes and V-neck. At this point, there should be 11 (13, 15, 17, 20) dc on each front and 30 (35, 40, 45, 48) dc on the back.

RIGHT FRONT
Shape armhole and V-neck at the same time.
Armhole shaping: Work 9 (11, 13, 15, 18) dc; turn. Decrease 1 dc at armhole edge on every row 2 times.
V-neck: Decrease 1 dc at neck edge on every row 4 (6, 8, 10, 12) times = 3 (3, 3, 3, 4) dc rem for shoulder.

Continue in pattern until total length measures 34 (34¾, 35½, 36¼, 37) in / 86 (88, 90, 92, 94) cm.

LEFT FRONT
Count 8 (10, 12, 14, 17) sts in from center front and attach yarn between it and the next dc = 9 (11, 13, 15, 18) dc. Work as for right front, reversing shaping to match.

BACK
With RS facing, skip 3 dc, attach yarn at next dc and work 28 (33, 38, 43, 46) dc; turn. Shape armhole at each side as for front and then continue in pattern until piece reaches total length. Sew or crochet to seam shoulder.

FRONT BAND
With RS facing, attach yarn at lower right corner. Ch 4 (= 1st dc + ch 1), (skip 1 dc or 3 ch, 3 dc around next dc or ch-3 loop, ch 1) up to shoulder seam. Along back neck, skip 3 sts, work 3 dc in next st. Work down left side as for right side and end with ch 1 and 1 dc in last st. Continue in Pattern B, beginning on Row 2, working a total of 6 rows.
Now work 1 rnd sc around entire outer edge of cardigan. Work 1 sc in each dc and 2 sc around each ch loop along front edges. At lower edge, work 4 sc around each ch loop and 1 sc in each st where 3 dc are worked into the same st.

SLEEVES
Ch 18 (21, 24, 24, 27); join into a ring with 1 sl st into 1st ch. Pm for beginning of rnd, moving marker up each rnd.
Rnd 1: Ch 3 and work 2 dc in 1st ch, (ch 1, skip 2 ch, 3 dc in next ch) around, ending with ch 1 and 1 sl st into 3rd ch at beg of rnd.
Rnds 2-8: 1 sl st around ch, ch 3, 2 dc around same ch, (ch 1, 3 dc around next ch) around, ending with ch 1 and 1 sl st into 3rd ch at beg of rnd.
Rnd 9: Ch 3 and then work 1 dc in each dc, skip ch. End with 1 sl st into 3rd ch at beg of rnd = 18 (21, 24, 24, 27) dc.
Rnd 10: Work around in Pattern A, beginning on Row 2, and increase 1 dc on each side of marker on every other rnd 7 (7, 7, 8, 8) times = 32 (35, 38, 40, 43) dc. Continue as est until sleeve measures 19 (19¼, 19¾, 19¾, 20) in / 48 (49, 50, 50, 51) cm.
Sleeve cap: On the next row, work 2 sl sts in the 1st 2 dc and then work as est until 2 sts before marker; turn. Now work back and forth.

Pattern A

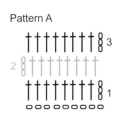

Pattern B

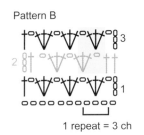

1 repeat = 3 ch

Chart Symbols

◯ = ch

† = dc

▨ = 1 repeat

Decrease 1 st at each side 9 (10, 10, 11, 11) times and then 2 sts at each side once.

FINISHING
Weave in all ends neatly on WS. Attach sleeves and gently steam press garment.

Black Poncho with Detachable Hood and Wrist Warmers

This poncho is quick to crochet, with a large hook and an easy-to-memorize pattern. The detachable hood is very practical: Wear it on its own as a cowl, or pull it up to make a hood when your ears get cold. If you'd rather make the hood by itself to use as a cowl, consider getting decorative and attaching fringe around the lower edge. And wrist warmers are always a great accessory for a poncho (or any other sleeveless garment) to help keep your arms comfortable!

LEVEL OF DIFFICULTY
Intermediate

SIZES
One size

FINISHED MEASUREMENTS
PONCHO
Length at center front: 40¼ in / 102 cm + fringe

WRIST WARMERS
Length: 8¾ in / 22 cm
Circumference: approx. 8 in / 20 cm

HOOD
Circumference at lower edge: 26¾ in / 68 cm
Length of hood only: 13¾ in / 35 cm

MATERIALS
Yarn:
CYCA #6 (super bulky), Garnstudio Drops Andes (65% wool, 35% alpaca, 105 yd/96 m / 100 g).

Yarn Color and Amounts:
Black 8903: poncho: 1100 g; hood/cowl: 300 g; wrist warmers: 100 g

Crochet Hook: U. S. M/N-13 / 9 mm for poncho and hood; U. S. size J-10 / 6 mm for wrist warmers

GAUGE
1 rep over 8 ch in Pattern A with larger hook = approx. 4¼ in / 11 cm.
Adjust hook size to obtain correct gauge if necessary.

PATTERN A (MULTIPLE OF 8 + 1 STS)

Row 1: Ch 1, 1 sc, (skip 3 ch, 9 dc in next ch, skip 3 ch, 1 sc in next ch) across.

Row 2: Ch 3 (= 1st dc) and 1 dc in sc, [ch 2, skip 4 dc, 1 sc in next dc, ch 2, (1 dc, ch 1, 1 dc) in next sc] across, ending with ch 2, skip 4 dc, 1 sc in next dc, ch 2, 2 dc in last sc.

Row 3: Ch 3 (= 1st dc) and 4 dc in 1st dc, (1 sc in sc, 9 dc around ch-1 loop) across, ending with 1 sc in sc and 5 dc in 3rd ch at beg of previous row.

Rnd 4: Ch 1, 1 sc in 1st dc, [ch 2, (1 dc, ch 1, 1 dc) in next sc, ch 2, skip 4 dc, 1 sc in next dc] across, ending with ch 2, (1 dc, ch 1, 1 dc) in next sc, ch 2, 1 sc in 3rd ch at beg of previous rnd.

Row 5: Ch 1, 1 sc in sc, (9 dc around ch-1 loop, 1 sc in next sc) across.
Rep Rows 2-5.

PATTERN B (MULTIPLE OF 2 STS)

Pm and move it up at beginning of each rnd; do not end rnd with sl st.

Rnd 1: Ch 1, 1 sc in 1st st, (ch 1, skip 1 st, 1 sc in next st) around.

Rnd 2: (1 sc around ch, ch 1, skip 1 sc) around.
Rep Rnd 2.

TIP

If you want a shorter poncho, begin with fewer chain stitches. The stitch count must be a multiple of 8 + 1 sts. Each repeat measures approx. 4¼ in / 11 cm, so the poncho will be 4¼ in / 11 cm shorter for each repeat you omit.

PONCHO

Ch 65 with hook U. S. M/N-13 / 9 mm. Work back and forth in Pattern A until piece measures approx. 52¾ in / 134 cm, ending with pattern Row 2 or 4. Fold piece in half = 26½ in / 67 cm for each half. Measure approx. 11 in / 28 cm down from the fold (= neck opening) and seam the piece from this point and down on WS.

Lower edge: Ch 1 and then work sc evenly spaced around the garment. Next, work 2 rnds Pattern B.

Neckband: Attach yarn at center back, ch 1 and work 2 rnds in sc, ending with 1 sl st into 1st sc.

Fringe: Cut 4 strands, 8¾ in / 22 cm long for each fringe bundle. Double the strands and attach with rug knot in every 3rd st all around the edge.

HOOD

Ch 65 with hook U. S. M/N-13 / 9 mm.
Beginning in 2nd ch from hook, work 1 sc in each ch, ending with 1 sl st into 1st sc. Continue around in Pattern B until piece measures 5¼ in / 13 cm.

Hood: Work Pattern A over 49 sts = 6 repeats. This leaves an opening at center front. Work back and forth until Pattern A section measures approx. 13¾ in / 35 cm. End with Row 2 or 4 of pattern.
Fold the hood in half and, with WS facing, seam the top edge.

Edging around hood: With RS facing, work 1 row sc along Pattern A. Working back and forth, work 6 rows Pattern B. Begin each row with ch 1 and 1 sc and end with 1 sc. Next, work 1 row with 1 sc in each sc. Fold edging out and tack it down with a few stitches at center of hood. Cut 10 strands each 9¾ in / 25 cm long, fold in half and attach at back tip of hood. Wrap yarn a few times at top of tassel and fasten off.

WRIST WARMERS

With hook U. S. size J-10 / 6 mm, ch 24 and join into a ring with 1 sl st into 1st ch.
Ch 1 and then work 1 sc in each ch. Work Pattern B in the round until piece measures 2¾ in / 7 cm and then change to Pattern A.

Rnd 1: Ch 1, (1 sc, skip 3 sts, 9 dc in next st, skip 3 sts) around, ending with 1 sl st into 1st sc.

Rnd 2: Ch 4 and work 1 dc in 1st sc, [ch 2, skip 4 dc, 1 sc in next dc, ch 2, (1 dc, ch 1, 1 dc) in next sc] around, ending with ch 2, skip 4 dc, 1 sc in next dc, ch 2, 1 sl st into 3rd ch at beg of rnd.

Rnd 3: 1 sl st around ch-1 loop, ch 3, 4 dc around ch-1 loop, (1 sc in sc, 9 dc around ch-1 loop) around, ending with 1 sc in sc, 4 dc around 1st ch-1 loop, 1 sl st into 3rd ch at beg of rnd.

Rnd 4: Ch 1, 1 sc, [ch 2, (1 dc, ch 1, 1 dc) in next sc, ch 2, skip 4 dc, 1 sc in next dc] around, ending with ch 2, (1 dc, ch 1, 1 dc) in next sc, ch 2, skip 4 dc, 1 sl st into 1st sc.

Rnd 5: Ch 1, 1 sc in sc, (9 dc around ch-1 loop, 1 sc in next sc) around, ending with 1 sl st into 1st sc.
Rep Rnds 2-5 until piece is approx. 8 in / 20 cm long, ending with Row 2 or 4 of Pattern A. Finish with a rnd of 1 sc in each st, ending rnd with 1 sl st into 1st sc.
Make another wrist warmer the same way. Use a hole in the pattern for thumbhole.

Pattern A

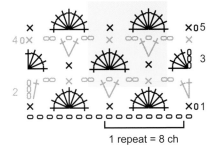

1 repeat = 8 ch

Pattern B

○ × ○ × ○ × ○ × ○ × ○ × × 3
× ○ × ○ × ○ × ○ × ○ × ○ × 2
○ × ○ × ○ × ○ × ○ × ○ × × 01
○ ○ ○ ○ ○ ○ ○ ○ ○ ○ ○ ○ ○

1 repeat = 2 ch

Chart Symbols

○ = ch

× = sc

† = dc

   = 1 repeat

Pink Sweater with Detached Collar

This sweater is worked only with double crochet, which makes for easy going. The leaf edging is fun, and you can wear the detached flower collar with other garments! Make the collar with stash yarn if you want. Be creative and make each flower with a different color— or use several colors for each flower.

LEVEL OF DIFFICULTY
Intermediate

SIZES
XS (S, M, L, XL, XXL)

FINISHED MEASUREMENTS
Chest: 37¼ (39½, 41¾, 44, 46½, 48¾) in / 94 (100, 106, 112, 118, 124) cm
Length: 20½ (21¼, 22, 22¾, 23¾, 24½) in / 52 (54, 56, 58, 60, 62) cm + 2 in / 5 cm edging
Sleeve length: 3¼ (3¼, 3¼, 3¼, 3¼ 3¼) in / 8 (8, 8, 8, 8, 8) cm + 2 in / 5 cm edging

COLLAR
SIZES
One size

FINISHED MEASUREMENTS
Circumference: 29½ in / 75 cm
Length: 14¼ in / 36 cm

MATERIALS
Yarn:
CYCA #3 (DK/light worsted), Sandnes Garn Mandarin Medi (100% cotton, 147 yd/134 m / 50 g)

Yarn Color and Amounts:
Light Pink 4301: 350 (400, 450, 500, 550, 600) g for the sweater and 150 g for collar

Crochet Hook: U. S. G-6 / 4 mm

GAUGE
14 dc and 11 rows = 4 x 4 in / 10 x 10 cm. 1 flower measures approx. 6 in / 15 cm in diameter.
Adjust hook size to obtain correct gauge if necessary.

Pattern

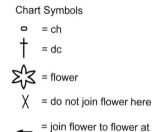

Chart Symbols

o = ch

† = dc

✳ = flower

✗ = do not join flower here

⟵ = join flower to flower at beginning of row

Joining with crochet

PATTERN

Row 1: Ch 1, 1 dc in each ch across.
Row 2: Ch 3, 1 dc between 1st and 2nd dc and then 1 dc between each dc across.
Rep Row 2.

LEAF EDGING

Attach yarn with 1 sl st. Work (ch 13, beg in 3rd ch from hook, work 1 sc, 1 hdc in next ch, 1 dc in each of next 2 ch, ch 3, skip 3 ch, 1 sl st in next ch, skip 4 dc on sweater, 1 sc between 2 dc) around, ending with 1 sl st into 1st sc.

SWEATER

BACK

Ch 68 (72, 76, 80, 84, 88) and work back and forth in Pattern. Continue as est until piece measures approx. 20 (21, 21¾, 22½, 23¼, 24) in / 51 (53, 55, 57, 59, 61) cm or 1 row before total desired length.
Back neck: Work 1 row over the 1st 21 (22, 23, 24, 25, 26) dc, cut yarn. Skip 26 (28, 30, 32, 34, 36) dc and attach yarn in next st, work in dc over last 21 (22, 23, 24, 25, 26) dc. Cut yarn and fasten off.

FRONT

Work as for back until it measures approx. 18¼ (19, 19¾, 20½, 21¼, 22) in / 46 (48, 50, 52, 54, 56) cm.
Neck: Work 6 rows over the 1st 21 (22, 23, 24, 25, 26) dc; cut yarn. Skip 26 (28, 30, 32, 34, 36) dc and attach yarn in next st. Work 6 rows over the last 21 (22, 23, 24, 25, 26) dc. Cut yarn and fasten off.

SLEEVES

Ch 56 (60, 64, 68, 72, 76). Work back and forth in Pattern until piece measures 3¼ in / 8 cm or desired length. Cut yarn and fasten off.

FINISHING

Weave in all ends neatly on WS. Sew or crochet shoulder seams. Pin center of sleeve top to shoulder seam. Pin sleeve down armhole, making sure armhole depth matches on each side. Sew or crochet to attach sleeves and then seam sides and sleeves.
Edging: Crochet the Leaf Edging around lower edge of sweater and ends of sleeves. Try to work the same number of leaves on front and back. You might need to skip 1 st more or less for the edging to be even. Begin at side seam of the body and center of underarm on sleeves.
Gently steam press under a damp pressing cloth.

COLLAR

Flower: Ch 4 and join into a ring with 1 sl st into 1st ch.
Rnd 1: Ch 3 (= 1st dc), work 11 dc around ring, 1 sl st into 3rd ch at beg of rnd.
Rnd 2: Ch 1 and work 1 sc into dc, (ch 11, turn; skip 1st ch, work 1 sc in next ch, 1 hdc in next ch, 1 dc in next ch, 1 tr in each of the next 2 ch, 1 dc in each of the next 2 ch, 1 hdc in next ch, 1 sc in each of the next 2 ch, 1 sl st in next dc of Rnd 1, 1 sc in next dc) 5 times, ch 11; turn. Skip 1st st, work 1 sc in next ch, 1 hdc in next ch, 1 dc in next ch, 1 tr in each of the next 2 ch, 1 dc in each of the next 2 ch, 1 hdc in next ch, 1 sc in each of the next 2 ch, 1 sl st in next dc of Rnd 1, 1 sl st in 1st sc of rnd = 6 flower petals.
Rnd 3: 1 sl st in each of the next 3 sts (to ch with 1 dc), (1 sc in each of the next 7 sts, 2 sc in sc at tip, 1 sc in each of next 7 sts down the opposite side, skip 7 sts and beg on next flower petal) 5 times, 1 sc in each of next 7 sts, 2 sc in sc at tip, 1 sc in each of next 7 sts down opposite side, 1 sl st in 1st sc.

Rnd 4: (1 hdc in each of next 7 sc, ch 3, 1 hdc in each of next 7 sc, sc2tog over the next 2 sc) 6 times, 1 sl st in 1st hdc.

JOINING
Crochet the flowers together on the last rnd. Instead of ch 3 at the tip of each petal, work ch 1, 1 sl st in previous flower and ch 1.

Crochet 15 flowers together following the chart. Weave in all ends neatly on WS. Note that the bottom row of petals is not joined so the collar will lie more smoothly.

Vest with Rounded Back

This vest only has one size but it is quite wide and elastic. If you want a larger vest, you can substitute Mandarin Medi which is slightly heavier than Mandarin Petit. The same size hook works with either yarn.

LEVEL OF DIFFICULTY
Advanced

SIZES
One size

FINISHED MEASUREMENTS
Length at center back: 33 in / 84 cm
Width: The circle on the back measures approx. 26½ in / 67 cm in diameter, each front measures 9¾ in / 25 cm including the 1½ in / 4 cm edging. Take measurements after completing all increases

MATERIALS
Yarn:
CYCA #1 (fingering), Sandnes Garn Mandarin Petit (100% cotton, 195 yd/178 m / 50 g):
Dusty Petroleum 6822: 300 g

Crochet Hook: U. S. E-4 / 3.5 mm

GAUGE
10 dc and 10 rows = 4 x 4 in / 10 x 10 cm.
Adjust hook size to obtain correct gauge if necessary.

TECHNIQUES
2-dc cl: 2 dc joined
3-dc cl: 3 dc joined
4-dc cl: 4 dc joined
For each cluster, work dc up to last step, work following dc also up to last step. Finish with yarn over hook and through all loops on hook.

Pattern on front and top of back

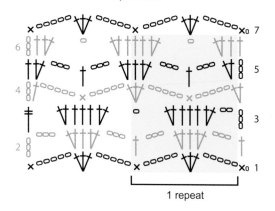

1 repeat

Chart Symbols

o = ch

✕ = sc

† = dc

╪ = tr

▨ = 1 repeat

Increases on front

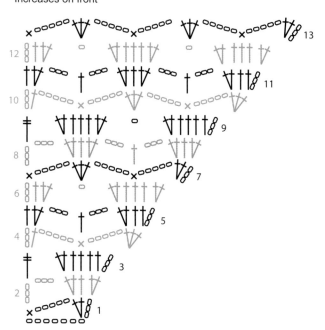

Neck shaping on front

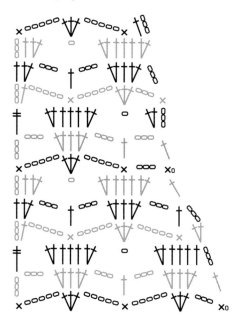

PATTERN ON FRONT (MULTIPLE OF 12 + 1 STS)
Row 1: Beg in 2nd ch from hook, work 1 sc, (ch 5, skip 5 sts, 3 dc in next st, ch 5, skip 5 sts, 1 sc in next st) across.
Row 2: Ch 6, (2 dc in 1st dc, 1 dc in next dc, 2 dc in next dc, ch 3, 1 dc in sc, ch 3) across, ending with 2 dc in 1st dc, 1 dc in next dc, 2 dc in next dc, ch 3, 1 dc in sc.
Row 3: Ch 5, (2 dc in next dc, 1 dc in each of next 3 dc, 2 dc in next dc, ch 1) across, ending with 2 dc in next dc, 1 dc in each of next 3 dc, 2 dc in next dc, 1 tr in 3rd ch at beg of previous row.
Row 4: Ch 3, 1 dc in tr, (ch 5, skip 3 dc, 1 sc in next

dc, ch 5, 3 dc around ch) across, ending with ch 5, skip 3 dc, 1 sc in next dc, ch 5, 2 dc in 5th ch at beg of previous row.
Row 5: Ch 3, 2 dc in next dc, (ch 3, 1 dc in sc, ch 3, 2 dc in next dc, 1 dc in next dc, 2 dc in next dc) across, ending with ch 3, 1 dc in sc, ch 3, 2 dc in next dc, 1 dc in 3rd ch at beg of previous row.
Row 6: Ch 3, 1 dc in next dc, 2 dc in next dc, (ch 1, 2 dc in next dc, 1 dc in each of the next 3 dc, 2 dc in next dc) across, ending with ch 1, 2 dc in next dc, 1 dc in next dc, 1 dc in 3rd ch at beg of previous row.
Row 7: Ch 1, 1 sc in 1st dc, (ch 5, 3 dc around next ch, ch 5, skip 3 dc, 1 sc in next dc) across, ending with

last sc in 3rd ch at beg of previous row.
Rep Rows 2-7.

BACK

Circle: Ch 8 and join into a ring with 1 sl st into 1st ch.

Rnd 1: Ch 4, work 23 tr around ring and end with 1 sl st into 4th ch = 24 tr.

Rnd 2: Ch 4 (= 1st dc + ch 1), (1 dc in next tr, ch 1) 23 times, 1 sl st into 3rd ch at beg of rnd.

Rnd 3: Ch 5 (= 1st dc + ch 2), (1 dc in next dc, ch 2) 23 times, 1 sl st into 3rd ch at beg of rnd.

Rnd 4: 1 sl st around 1st ch-2 loop, ch 3 and work 1 3-dc cl around ch-2 loop, (4-dc cl around next ch-2 loop, ch 3) 23 times, 1 sl st into 1st dc cl.

Rnd 5: 1 sl st around 1st ch-3 loop, ch 3, 3 dc around same ch-3 loop, [(4 dc around next ch-3 loop, 1 dc in dc cl) 3 times, ch 1] 7 times, 1 sl st into 3rd ch at beg of rnd.

Rnd 6: 1 sl st in next dc, ch 3, 1 dc in each of next 12 dc, ch 3, skip 1 dc + 1 ch + 1 dc, (1 dc in each of next 13 dc, ch 3, skip 1 dc + 1 ch + 1 dc) 7 times, 1 sl st in 3rd ch at beg of rnd.

Rnd 7: 1 sl st in next dc, ch 3, 1 dc in each of next 10 dc, ch 4, skip 1 dc + 3 ch + 1 dc, (1 dc in each of next 11 dc, ch 4, skip 1 dc + 3 ch + 1 dc) 7 times, 1 sl st in 3rd ch at beg of rnd.

Rnd 8: 1 sl st in next dc, ch 3, 1 dc in each of next 8 dc, ch 4, skip 1 dc + 1 ch, 1 dc in each of next 2 ch, ch 4, skip 1 dc + 1 ch, (1 dc in each of next 9 dc, ch 4, skip 1 ch + 1 dc, 1 dc in each of next 2 ch, ch 4, skip 1 ch + 1 dc) 7 times, 1 sl st in 3rd ch at beg of rnd.

Rnd 9: 1 sl st in next dc, ch 3, 1 dc in each of next 6 dc, ch 5, 1 dc around ch-4 loop, 1 dc in each of next 2 dc, 1 dc around ch-4 loop, ch 5, skip 1 dc, (1 dc in each of next 7 dc, ch 5, 1 dc around ch-4 loop, 1 dc in each of next 2 dc, 1 dc around ch-4 loop, ch 5, skip 1 dc) 7 times, 1 sl st in 3rd ch at beg of rnd.

Rnd 10: 1 sl st in next dc, 1 dc in each of next 5 dc, ch 6, 1 dc around ch-5 loop, 1 dc in each of next 4 dc, 1 dc around ch-5 loop, ch 6, skip 1 dc, (1 dc in each of next 5 dc, ch 6, 1 dc around ch-5 loop, 1 dc in each of next 4 dc, 1 dc around ch-5 loop, ch 6, skip 1 dc) 7 times, 1 sl st in 3rd ch at beg of rnd.

Rnd 11: 1 sl st in next dc, ch 3, 2-dc cl over next 2 dc, ch 3, skip 1 dc + 2 ch, 1 dc in each of next 2 ch, ch 3, skip 2 ch + 1 dc, 1 dc in each of next 4 dc, ch 3, skip 1 dc + 2 ch, 1 dc in each of next 2 ch, ch 3, skip 2 ch + 1 dc, (3-dc cl over next 3 dc, ch 3, skip 1 dc + 2 ch, 1 dc in each of next 2 ch, ch 3, skip 2 ch + 1 dc, 1 dc in each of next 4 dc, ch 3, skip 1 dc + 2 ch, 1 dc in each of next 2 ch, ch 3, skip 2 ch + 1 dc) 7 times, 1 sl

st in 1st dc cl.

Rnd 12: Ch 7 (= 1st dc + ch 4), 1 dc around ch-3 loop, 1 dc in each of next 2 dc, 1 dc around ch-3 loop, ch 4, skip 1 dc, 1 dc in each of next 2 dc, ch 4, 1 dc around ch-3 loop, 1 dc in each of next 2 dc, 1 dc around ch-3 loop, ch 4, (1 dc in dc cl, ch 4, 1 dc around ch-3 loop, 1 dc in each of the next 2 dc, 1 dc around ch-3 loop, ch 4, skip 1 dc, 1 dc in each of next 2 dc, ch 4, 1 dc around ch-3 loop, 1 dc in each of next 2 dc, 1 dc around ch-3 loop, ch 4) 7 times, 1 sl st in 3rd ch at beg of rnd.

Rnd 13: Ch 8 (= 1st dc + ch 5), skip ch-4 loop + 1 dc, 1 dc in each of next dc, ch 5, skip ch-4 loop + 1 dc, 1 dc in next dc, ch 5, skip ch-4 loop + 1 dc, 1 dc in each of next 2 dc, ch 5, (1 dc in dc, ch 5, skip ch-4 loop + 1 dc, 1 dc in each of next 2 dc, ch 5, skip ch loop + 1 dc, 1 dc in next dc, ch 5, skip ch-4 loop + 1 dc, 1 dc in each of next 2 dc, ch 5) 7 times, 1 sl st in 3rd ch at beg of rnd.

Rnd 14: Ch 9 (= 1st dc + ch 6), skip ch-5 loop + 1 dc, 1 dc in next dc, ch 6, 1 dc in next dc, ch 6, skip ch-5 loop + 1 dc, 1 dc in next dc, ch 6, (1 dc in next dc, ch 6, skip ch-5 loop + 1 dc, 1 dc in next dc, ch 6, 1 dc in next dc, ch 6, skip ch-5 loop + 1 dc, 1 dc in next dc, ch 6) 7 times, 1 sl st in 3rd ch at beg of rnd.

Rnd 15: Ch 3, 9 dc around ch-6 loop, (1 dc in next dc, 9 dc around ch-6 loop) 31 times, 1 sl st in 3rd ch at beg of rnd.

Rnd 16: [(Ch 3, 1 dc, ch 3, 2 dc) in 1st dc, ch 3, skip 9 dc, (2 dc, ch 3, 2 dc) in next dc, ch 3, skip 9 dc] 31 times, 1 sl st in 3rd ch at beg of rnd.

Rnd 17: Sl st to ch-3 loop, (ch 3, 1 dc, ch 3, 2 dc) around ch-3 loop, ch 4, skip 2 dc + 3 ch + 2 dc, [(2 dc, ch 3, 2 dc) around ch-3 loop, ch 4, skip 2 dc + 3 ch + 2 dc] 31 times, 1 sl st in 3rd ch at beg of rnd.

Rnd 18: Work as for Rnd 17 but with ch 5 instead of ch 4.

Rnd 19: Work as for Rnd 18 but with ch 6 instead of ch 5.

Rnd 20: Work as for Rnd 19 but with ch 7 instead of ch 6.

Rnd 21: Work as for Rnd 20 but with ch 8 instead of ch 7.

Rnd 22: Sl st to ch-3 loop, ch 3, 2 dc around ch-3 loop, ch 1, 8 dc around ch-7 loop, ch 1, (3 dc around next ch-3 loop, ch 1, 8 dc around ch-7 loop, ch 1) 31 times, 1 sl st in 3rd ch at beg of rnd.

Rnd 23: 1 sl st in next dc, (ch 3, 1 dc, ch 3, 2 dc) in same dc, ch 4, skip 1 dc + 1 ch + 3 dc, 1 dc in each of next 2 dc, ch 4, skip 3 dc + 1 ch + 1 dc, [(2 dc, ch 3, 2 dc) in next dc, ch 4, skip 1 dc + 1 ch + 3 dc, 1 dc in each of the next 2 dc, ch 4, skip 3 dc + 1 ch + 1 dc] 31 times, 1 sl st in 3rd ch at beg of rnd.

Rnd 24: Sl st to ch-3 loop, (ch 3, 1 dc, ch 3, 2 dc) around ch-3 loop, ch 4, 1 dc around ch-4 loop, 1 dc in each of next 2 dc, 1 dc around ch-4 loop, ch 4, skip 2 dc [(2 dc, ch 3, 2 dc) around ch-3 loop, ch 4, 1 dc around ch-4 loop. 1 dc in each of next 2 dc, 1 dc around ch-4 loop, ch 4, skip 2 dc] 31 times, 1 sl st in 3rd ch at beg of rnd.

Rnd 25: Sl st to ch-3 loop, (ch 3, 1 dc, ch 3, 2 dc) around ch-3 loop, ch 4, skip ch loop, 1 dc in each of next 4 dc, ch 4, skip ch loop + 2 dc, [(2 dc, ch 3, 2 dc) around ch-3 loop, ch 4, skip ch-4 loop, 1 dc in each of next 4 dc, ch 4, skip ch-4 loop + 2 dc] 31 times, 1 sl st in 3rd ch at beg of rnd.

Rnds 26-27: Work as for Rnd 25 but ch 5 and (Rnd 27) 6 instead of ch 4.

Rnd 28: Sl st to ch-3 loop, (ch 3, 1 dc, ch 3, 2 dc) around ch-3 loop, ch 6, skip 2 dc + ch-6 loop + 1 dc, 1 dc in each of next 2 dc, ch 6, skip 1 dc + ch-6 loop + 2 dc, [(2 dc, ch 3, 2 dc) around ch-3 loop, ch 6, skip 2 dc + ch-6 loop + 1 dc, 1 dc in each of next 2 dc, ch 6, skip 1 dc + ch-6 loop + 2 dc] 31 times, 1 sl st in 3rd ch at beg of rnd.

Rnd 29: Sl st to ch-3 loop, ch 3, 2 dc around ch-3 loop, 6 dc around ch-6 loop, skip 1 dc, 1 dc in next dc, 6 dc around ch-6 loop, (3 dc around ch-3 loop, 6 dc around ch-6 loop, skip 1 dc, 1 dc in next dc, 6 dc around ch-6 loop) 31 times, 1 sl st in 3rd ch at beg of rnd.

Top of back: Sl st to ch-3 loop. Work back and forth in Pattern over the 5 rep at top of circle = 7 rep per row. Work 5 rows. If you want a longer back, add a few more rows before shaping back neck.

Back neck: Work over the 1st 2½ rep and fasten off. Work opposite shoulder the same way.

RIGHT FRONT

Work back and forth in Pattern, increasing at right side (follow the instructions below of the chart).

Row 1: Work 2 dc in 3rd ch from hook, ch 5, 1 sc in last ch.

Row 2: Ch 6, 2 dc in 1st dc, 1 dc in next dc, 2 dc in 3rd ch of previous row.

Row 3: Ch 3, 1 dc in 1st dc, 1 dc in each of next 3 dc, 2 dc in next dc, 1 tr in 3rd ch at beg of previous row.

Row 4: Ch 3, 1 dc in tr, ch 5, skip 3 dc, 1 sc in next dc, ch 5, 3 dc around ch of previous row.

Row 5: Ch 3, 1 dc in 1st dc, 1 dc in next dc, 2 dc in next dc, ch 3, 1 dc in sc, ch 3, 2 dc in next dc, 1 dc in 3rd ch of previous row.

Row 6: Ch 3, 1 dc in next dc, 2 dc in next dc, ch 1, skip 3 ch + 1 dc + 3 ch, 2 dc in next dc, 1 dc in each of next 3 dc, 2 dc in 3rd ch of previous row.

Row 7: Ch 3, 2 dc in 1st dc, ch 5, skip 2 dc, 1 sc in next dc, ch 5, 3 dc around ch, ch 5, skip 3 dc, 1 sc in 3rd ch of previous row.

Row 8: Ch 6, 2 in in 1st dc, 1 dc in next dc, 2 dc in next dc, ch 3, 1 dc in sc, ch 3, 2 dc in next dc, 1 dc in next dc, 2 dc in 3rd ch of previous row.

Row 9: Ch 3, 1 dc in 1st dc, 1 dc in each of next 3 dc, 2 dc in next dc, ch 1, skip 3 ch + 1 dc + 3 ch, 2 dc in next dc, 1 dc in each of next 3 dc, 2 dc in next dc, 1 tr in 3rd ch of previous row.

Row 10: Ch 3, 1 dc in tr, ch 5, skip 3 dc, 1 sc in next dc, ch 5, 3 dc around ch, ch 5, skip 3 dc, 1 sc in next dc, ch 5, 3 dc in 3rd ch of previous row.

Row 11: Ch 3, 1 dc in 1st dc, 1 dc in next dc, 2 dc in next dc, ch 3, 1 dc in sc, ch 3, 2 dc in next dc, 1 dc in next dc, 2 dc in next dc, ch 3, 1 dc in sc, ch 3, 2 dc in next dc, 1 dc in 3rd ch of previous row.

Row 12: Ch 3, 1 dc in 1st dc, 2 dc in next dc, ch 1, skip 3 ch + 1 dc + 3 ch, 2 dc in next dc, 1 dc in each of next 3 dc, 2 dc in next dc, skip 3 ch + 1 dc + 3 ch, 2 dc in next dc, 1 dc in each of next 3 dc, 2 dc in 3rd ch of previous row.

Row 13: Ch 3, 2 dc in 1st dc, ch 5, skip 2 dc, 1 sc in next dc, ch 5, 3 dc around ch, ch 5, skip 3 dc, 1 sc in next dc, ch 5, 3 dc around ch, 5 ch, skip 3 dc, 1 sc in 3rd ch of previous row.

Increase as est until there are 5½ rep. Continue without further shaping and beg / end rows at the left side as shown on the chart. End when piece measures approx. 23¼ in / 59 cm at the left side, ending with Row 6 of pattern. If you have lengthened the back, lengthen the front correspondingly.

Neck shaping: Decrease at right side as shown on the chart until 2½ rep rem. End when piece measures approx. 31½ in / 80 cm at the left side; cut yarn and fasten off.

LEFT FRONT

Work as for right front.

FINISHING

Weave in all ends neatly on WS. Sew or crochet shoulder seams. Measure down 9 in / 23 cm down from shoulder seam at right side. The side seam begins here. Sew the front pieces to the back with the front flat but a little loose along the back. Rep on the left side, making sure that you begin and end the seaming at the same place as for right front.

EDGING AROUND THE VEST (MULTIPLE OF 6 STS)

Rnd 1: Attach yarn at a side seam with 1 sl st. Ch 1 and then work around the vest in sc, with approx. 3 sc around each dc along the front pieces and 1 sc in each dc along the back. Make sure the sts are evenly distributed around. End with 1 sl st into 1st sc.

Rnd 2: Ch 4 (= 1st dc + ch 1), skip 1 sc, (1 dc in next sc, ch 1, skip 1 sc) around, ending with 1 sl st in 3rd ch at beg of rnd.

Rnd 3: Ch 1, 1 sc in 1st dc, [ch 3, skip 1 ch, (1 sc in next dc, 1 sc around next ch) 2 times, 1 sc in next dc] around, ending with 1 sl st in 1st sc.

Rnd 4: This rnd is worked back and forth at the same time as you work firmly along the edge. If you follow the pattern, the tension will be correct. 1 sl st to ch-3 loop, ch 1, 1 sc around ch loop, ch 7, 1 dc in sc you just worked, [ch 3, 4 dc in dc you just worked, 1 sc in next ch-3 loop; turn. 1 sl st in each of the next 4 dc and 3rd ch; turn. Ch 3, skip 5 sl sts, 1 dc in sc (which was worked in ch-3 loop)] around. End with ch 3, 4 dc in the dc you just worked, and then use sl st to seam the short ends at beg of edging.

Sweater Dress and Hat

This sweater dress with three-quarter length sleeves is worked in double crochet with a pretty cotton/linen yarn. The hat is the perfect cherry on top, so to speak! The wide brim can be folded up at the side or center front depending on which look you prefer—and if you want a narrower brim instead, just end when you think it's wide enough for you.

LEVEL OF DIFFICULTY
Intermediate

DRESS
SIZES
S (M, L, XL)

FINISHED MEASUREMENTS
Chest: 36¼ (39½, 42½, 45¾) in / 92 (100, 108, 116) cm
Total length: 31½ (32¼, 33, 34) in / 80 (82, 84, 86) cm
Sleeve length, cuff to underarm: 10¼ (10¾, 11, 11½) in / 26 (27, 28, 29) cm

HAT
SIZE
One size

FINISHED MEASUREMENTS
Circumference: approx. 20½ in / 52 cm

MATERIALS
Yarn:
CYCA #4 (worsted/afghan/Aran), Sandnes Garn Line

(53% cotton, 33% other, 14% linen, 120 yd/110 m / 50 g)

Yarn Colors and Amounts:
SWEATER
Natural 1012: 500 (550, 600, 650) g
Terracotta 4234: 50 (50, 50, 50) g
Maize 2124: 50 (50, 50, 50) g

HAT
Terracotta 4234: 250 g
Natural 1012: small amount
Maize 2124: small amount

Crochet Hook: U. S. H-8 / 5 mm for the sweater and U.S. size G-6 / 4 mm for the hat

GAUGE
13 dc and 9 rows in Pattern with larger hook = approx. 4 x 4 in / 10 x 10 cm.
14 sc with doubled yarn and smaller hook = 4 in / 10 cm.
Adjust hook size to obtain correct gauge if necessary.

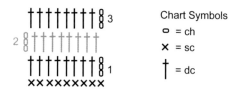

Chart Symbols

$\circ$ = ch

$\times$ = sc

$\dagger$ = dc

PATTERN

Row 1: Ch 3 in 1st sc and then work 1 dc in each sc across.

Row 2: Ch 2, 1 dc between the 1st and 2nd dc, 1 dc between the next 2 dc across.

Rep Row 2.

TIP FOR DECREASING

When decreasing at the beginning of a row, work a slip stitch over each stitch to be decreased. At the end of a row, turn, leaving stitches to be decreased unworked.

TIP FOR INCREASING

Work 2 stitches into the same stitch.

SWEATER DRESS

BACK

With Terracotta and hook U. S. H-8 / 5 mm, ch 66 (71, 76, 81).

Row 1: Beg in 2nd ch from hook, work 1 sc in each ch = 65 (70, 75, 80) sc.

Rows 2-3: Ch 1 and then work 1 sc in each sc across.

Row 4: Change to Maize and work as for Row 2 but, *at the same time*, skip 5 sc evenly spaced across = 60 (65, 70, 75) sc rem.

Change to Natural and work in Pattern until piece measures 23¾ (24, 24½, 24¾) in / 60 (61, 62, 63) cm. If you want a longer or shorter dress, adjust length at this point.

Armhole shaping: At each side on every row, decrease 3-2-1 sts. Continue in Pattern until piece measures 30¼ (31, 32, 33½) in / 77 (79, 81, 85) cm or 3 rows before total length.

Back neck: Work 11 (12, 13, 14) dc; turn. 1 sl st in next dc and complete row; turn. Work 9 (10, 11, 12) dc and fasten off. Skip the center 26 (29, 32, 35) dc and attach yarn in next dc. Work 11 (12, 13, 14) dc; turn. Work 10 (11, 12, 13) dc; turn. 1 sl st in next dc, 9 (10, 11, 12) dc; cut yarn and fasten off.

FRONT

Work as for back until piece measures 28¼ (29¼, 30, 30¾) in / 72 (74, 76, 78) cm or 7 rows before total length.

Neck: Work 18 (19, 20, 21) dc; turn. At neck edge, on every row, decrease 3-2-1-1-1-1 sts. Work 1 row and fasten off = 9 (10, 11, 12) dc. Skip the center 12 (15, 18, 21) dc and attach yarn on next dc. Shape neck as for opposite side.

SLEEVES

With Terracotta, ch 36 (40, 44, 48).

Row 1: Beginning in 2nd ch from hook, work 1 sc in each ch = 35 (39, 43, 47) sc.

Rows 2-3: Ch 1 and then work 1 sc in each sc across.

Row 4: Change to Maize and work as for Row 2 but, *at the same time*, skip 3 sc evenly spaced across = 32 (36, 40, 44) sc rem.

Change to Natural and work in Pattern, *at the same time*, shaping sleeve at each side:

Sleeve shaping: Increase 1 st at each side on every 5th row 3 times = 38 (42, 44, 48) dc. Work in pattern until sleeve measures 10¼ (10¾, 11, 11½) in / 26 (27, 28, 29) cm or desired length.

Sleeve cap: Decrease at each side on every row 3 sts 1 time, 2 sts 2 times, 1 st 3 (4, 5, 6) times, 2 sts 1 time, and 3 sts 1 time.

FINISHING

Weave in all ends neatly on WS. Sew or crochet shoulder, side, and sleeve seams.

Neckband:

Rnd 1: Attach Natural at right shoulder seam. Ch 1 and then work in sc evenly spaced around neck, ending with 1 sl st in 1st sc.

Rnd 2: Change to Maize, ch 1 and then work 1 sc in each sc around, ending with 1 sl st into 1st sc.

Rnds 3-5: Change to Terracotta and work as for Rnd 2. Cut yarn and fasten off.

Sew or crochet sleeves to attach to body.

HAT

The hat is crocheted in the round from the top down. With 2 strands of Terracotta held together and hook U. S. size G-6 / 4 mm, work in a spiral = do not join with sl st between rounds. Pm and move it up at beginning of rnd.

Ch 4 and join into a ring with 1 sl st into 1st ch.

Rnd 1: Ch 1, 5 sc around ring.

Rnd 2: Work 2 sc in each sc around = 10 sc.

Rnd 3: Work (2 sc in 1st sc, 1 sc in next sc) around = 15 sc.

Rnd 4: (2 sc in 1st sc, 1 sc in each of next 2 sc) around = 20 sc.

Rnd 5: (2 sc in 1st sc, 1 sc in each of next 3 sc) around = 25 sc.

Rnds 6-15: Work as for Rnd 5 but with 1 st more between each increase on each rnd = 80 sc on Rnd 15. Now work 1 sc in each sc without increasing until piece measures 6¼ in / 16 cm.

Brim:

Rnd 1: Work (1 sc in each of next 9 sc, 2 sc in next sc) around = 88 sc.

Rnd 2: Work 1 sc in each sc around.

Rnd 3: Work (1 sc in each of next 10 sc, 2 sc in next sc) around = 96 sc.

Rnd 4: Work 1 sc in each sc around.

Rep Rnds 3-4, increasing as before with 1 st more between each increase until brim measures approx. 4 in / 10 cm. End with 1 rnd sc without increasing

and 1 sl st into 1st sc of rnd. Cut yarn and fasten off.

BOW

With Natural, ch 30 and join into a ring with 1 sl st into 1st ch.

Rnds 1-4: Ch 1, 1 sc in each st around, ending with 1 sl st into 1st sc.

Rnd 5: Change to Maize and work as for Rnd 4.

Cut yarn and attach it at foundation chain. Ch 1, 1 sc in each ch around, ending with 1 sl st into 1st sc; cut yarn.

With Maize, ch 6. Beg in 2nd ch from hook, work 1 sc in each of the next 4 ch, 3 sc in last ch. Turn and work along bottom of foundation chain with 1 sc in each of the next 4 ch and 2 sc in last ch. Join the short ends with a sl st to form a ring; cut yarn. Fasten off yarn ends. Pull ring around the center of the bow.

Sew the bow securely to the hat or attach it with a safety pin so you can easily take it off in case you want to wear the hat without the bow.

Colorful Blanket and Pillow

This colorful set will keep you in good cheer! If you make it a little smaller, it'll be a lovely baby blanket. You can also use softer colors for an entirely different look. Play with different combinations and see what you like best.

LEVEL OF DIFFICULTY
Advanced

FINISHED MEASUREMENTS
Pillow: 15¾ x 23¾ in / 40 x 60 cm without edging
Blanket: approx. 37¾ x 64¼ in / 96 x 163 cm including edging

MATERIALS
Yarn:
CYCA #2 (sport/baby), Dale Garn Falk (100% wool, 116 yd/106 m / 50 g).

Yarn Colors and Amounts:
Falk:
Pink 4516: 700 g
Orange 3418: 200 g
Sun Yellow 2427: 200 g
Turquoise 5815: 300 g
Purple 5144: 50 g
CYCA #2 (sport/baby), Rauma PT 5 (80% wool, 20% nylon, 140 yd/128 m / 50 g):

PT 5: 100 g

Notions: Insert pillow 15¾ x 23¾ in / 40 x 60 cm

Crochet Hook: U. S. E-4 / 3.5 mm

GAUGE
Rnds 1-3 of a square measure approx. 2¾ x 4¾ in / 7 x 12 cm.
Adjust hook size to obtain correct gauge if necessary.

NOTE: The squares are joined in strips on the last round. Lightly steam press the strips and edging before joining the strips in single crochet from RS.

TIP
When changing colors, it will look best if you change to the new color on the last yarn around hook on the round with the old color.

SQUARE 1, WHOLE SQUARE

With Yellow, ch 6 and join into a ring with 1 sl st into 1st ch.

Rnd 1: Ch 1, (1 sc, 1 hdc, 1 dc, 1 tr, ch 3, 1 tr, 1 dc, 1 hdc, 1 sc, ch 1) around ring 2 times, 1 sl st in 1st sc.

Rnd 2, Orange: Ch 3 (= 1st dc), 1 dc in each of next 3 sts, (1 dc, 2 tr, ch 3, 2 tr, 1 dc) around ch-3 loop, 1 dc in each of next 4 sts, (1 dc, 2 tr, ch 3, 2 tr, 1 dc) around ch-3 loop, 1 dc in each of next 4 sts, ch 1, skip 1 ch, 1 sl st in 3rd ch.

Rnd 3, Pink: Ch 3, 1 dc in each of next 6 sts, (1 dc, 2 tr, ch 3, 2 tr, 1 dc) around ch-3 loop, 1 dc in each of next 7 sts, (1 dc, ch 1, 1 dc) around ch-1 loop, 1 dc in each of next 7 sts, (1 dc, 2 tr, ch 3, 2 tr, 1 dc) around ch-3 loop, 1 dc in each of next 7 sts, (1 dc, ch 1, 1 dc) around ch-1 loop, 1 sl st in 3rd ch.

Rnd 4, Turquoise: Ch 1, [1 sc around ch-1 loop, ch 5, skip 2 sts, (1 sc in next st, ch 5, skip 3 sts) 2 times, 1 sc in next st, ch 5, skip ch-3 loop, (1 sc in next st, ch 5, skip 3 sts) 2 times, 1 sc, ch 5, skip 2 dc], 2 times, 1 sl st in 1st sc.

SQUARE 2, WHOLE SQUARE

Work as for Square 1 but work Rnd 1 with Orange and Rnd 2 with Yellow.

SQUARE 3, SQUARE SPLIT LENGTHWISE

With Yellow, ch 6 and join into a ring with 1 sl st into 1st ch.

Always change to a new color in the right corner with RS facing on each row.

Row 1, Orange: Ch 1, 1 sc, 1 hdc, 1 dc, 1 tr, ch 3, 1 tr, 1 dc, 1 hdc, 1 sc around ring.

Row 2, Orange: Ch 3 (= 1st dc) and 1 dc in 1st st, 1 dc in each of next 3 sts, (1 dc, 2 tr, ch 3, 2 tr, 1 dc) around ch-3 loop, 1 dc in each of next 3 sts, 2 dc in last st.

Row 3, Pink: Ch 3 (= 1st dc) and 2 dc in 1st st, 1 dc in each of next 7 sts, (1 dc, 2 tr, ch 3, 2 tr, 1 dc) around ch-3 loop, 1 dc in each of next 7 sts, 3 dc in last st.

Row 4, Turquoise: Ch 1 and 1 sc in 1st st, (ch 5, skip 3 sts, 1 sc in next st) 3 times, ch 5, skip ch-3 loop, (1 sc in next st, ch 5, skip 3 sts) 3 times, 1 sc in last st.

SQUARE 4, SQUARE SPLIT LENGTHWISE

Work as for Square 3, but work Rnd 1 with Orange and Rnd 2 with Yellow.

SQUARE 5, SQUARE ON DIAGONAL

With Yellow, ch 6 and join into a ring with 1 sl st into 1st ch.

Always change to a new color in the right corner with RS facing on each row.

Row 1: Ch 4 (= 1st tr), 2 tr, 1 dc, 1 hdc, 1 sc, ch 1, 1 sc, 1 hdc, 1 dc, 3 tr around ring.

Row 2, Orange: Ch 3 (= 1st dc) and 2 dc in 1st st, 1 dc in each of next 5 sts, ch 1, skip 1 ch, 1 dc in each of next 5 sts, 3 dc in last st.

Row 3, Pink: Ch 3 (= 1st dc) and 2 dc in 1st st, 1 dc in each of next 7 sts, (1 dc, ch 1, 1 dc) around ch-1 loop, 1 dc in each of next 7 sts, 3 dc in last st.

Row 4, Turquoise: Ch 1, 1 sc in 1st dc, (ch 5, skip 3 dc, 1 sc in next st) 2 times, ch 5, skip 2 dc, 1 sc around ch-1 loop, ch 5, skip 2 sts, 1 sc in next st, (ch 5, skip 3 dc, 1 sc in next st) 2 times.

SQUARE 6, QUARTER SQUARE

With Yellow, ch 6 and join into a ring with 1 sl st into 1st ch.

Always change to a new color in the right corner with RS facing on each row.

Row 1: Ch 4 (= 1st tr), 2 tr, 1 dc, 1 hdc, 1 sc, around ring.

Row 2, Orange: Ch 4 (= 1st tr) and 2 tr in 1st st, 1 dc in each of next 5 sts.

Row 3, Pink: Ch 4 (= 1st tr), 2 tr in 1st st, 1 dc in each of next 6 sts, 2 dc in last st.

Row 4, Turquoise: Ch 1, 1 sc in 1st dc, (ch 5, skip 3 dc, 1 sc in next st) 2 times, ch 5, skip 2 dc, 1 sc in last st.

JOINING

On the 4th rnd/row work as follows in the top ch loop: ch 2, 1 sc around corresponding ch loop of previous square, ch 2, 1 sc in 1st tr of current square.

FLOWER EDGING

With Pink, ch 10.

Row 1: Ch 3 (= 1st dc), 1 dc in next st, ch 1, skip 1 st, 1 dc in next st, ch 1, skip 1 st, 1 dc in each of last 2 sts; turn.

Row 2: Ch 3 (= 1st dc), 1 dc in each of next 6 sts = 7 dc; turn.

Row 3: Ch 10, 1 sl st in 5th ch from hook, (ch 3, 2 dc around ring, ch 3, 1 sl st around ring) 4 times, ch 5, 1 dc in each of 1st 2 dc, ch 1, skip 1 dc, 1 dc in next dc, ch 1, skip 1 dc, 1 dc in last 2 dc; turn.

Row 4: Ch 3 (= 1st dc), 1 dc in each of next 6 sts = 7 dc; turn.

Row 5: Ch 5, 1 sl st in 3rd ch from hook, (ch 3, 1 sl st in same st) 2 times, ch 2, 1 dc in each of 1st 2 dc, ch 1, skip 1 dc, 1 dc in next dc, ch 1, skip 1 dc, 1 dc in each

of last 2 dc; turn.
Rep Rows 2-5.

BLANKET

Make 45 of Square 1; 54 of Square 2; 5 of Square 3; 6 of Square 4; 18 of Square 5; and 2 of Square 6. Following the schematic, crochet the squares together on the 4th rnd in strips of 9 whole squares and 1 half square split lengthwise.

Next, with Turquoise, work 1 rnd in sc all around each strip. Work 1 sc in each sc and 3 sc around each ch loop, but on the ch loops at the top and bottom of the strip, work 5 sc.

Gently steam press strips.

Now place the strips with WS facing WS, and, with Crab Apple Green and RS facing, crochet them together with sc. Rep until all the strips have been joined.

With Turquoise, work 2 rnds sc evenly spaced around the entire blanket, with approx. 3 sc around each dc and 3 sc in each corner. Make sure the edging is smooth and even.

Crochet the Flower Edging until it is approx. 5½ yd / 5 meters long or it reaches entirely around the blanket. With RS facing and Turquoise, work 1 row sc along top edge, with approx. 3 sc around each dc, or fewer if needed to keep the edging smooth. Place the edging WS facing WS with the blanket, easing it well at the corners, and pin together. Crochet the edging and blanket together with 1 rnd sc and Purple. Weave in all ends neatly on WS. Gently steam press.

PILLOW

Make 24 each of Squares 1 and 2 = 48 squares. Crochet the squares together on the 4th rnd, following the schematic. The last square on the strip is joined to the first square.

With Turquoise, work 1 rnd sc around the entire length. Work 1 sc in each sc and 3 sc in each ch loop. Gently steam press the pieces. Place the strips WS facing WS as shown in the drawing, and, with RS facing, crochet them together with Crab Apple Green and sc. Leave an opening for the insert pillow.

Now work 1 row of ch loops on each side where the Flower Edging will be attached. Crochet along each short side, centered on the squares. Attach Tur-

Joining the blanket

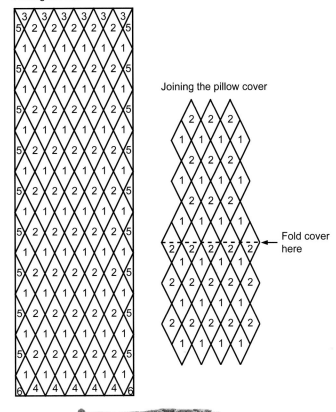

Joining the pillow cover

Fold cover here

quoise in a corner with the back facing you, work 1 sc, (ch 3, 1 sc around ch loop on Rnd 3 of square, ch 3, 1 sc around ch loop on Rnd 2, ch 3, 1 sc around ch loop on Rnd 1, ch 3, 1 sc in ring, ch 3, 1 sc on other side of ring, ch 3, 1 sc around ch loop on Rnd 1, ch 3, 1 sc around ch loop of Rnd 2, ch 3, 1 sc around ch loop on Rnd 3 of square, ch 3, 1 sc in join of 2 squares) to next corner; turn and work 3 sc in each ch loop back. Rep along the other short side. Make a Flower Edging approx. 15¾ in / 40 cm long. With Turquoise and RS facing, work 1 row sc along top edge, alternating 2 and 3 sc around each dc. Place the edge with WS facing back of cover and crochet the edge and cover together with Purple and 1 row sc. Weave in all ends neatly on WS. Gently steam press. Insert pillow and crochet opening to close.

Two Round Pillows

Your mother or grandmother might have made similar pillows for the sofa many years ago! Now you can try a fresh new design with bright colors. If you want a more neutral look, you can try beige, white, and yellow, for example—or a few different shades of the same color. Each cover is made like a tube to pull over the pillow, and then each end is tightened to close the ends. This is a great stash yarn project.

125

TIP
When changing colors, it will look best if you change to the new color on the last yarn around hook of the round with the old color.

LEVEL OF DIFFICULTY
Intermediate

BLUE AND WHITE PILLOW

FINISHED MEASUREMENTS
15¾ in / 40 cm in diameter

MATERIALS
Yarn:
CYCA #3 (DK/light worsted), Dale Garn Gullfasan

(90% rayon, 10% nylon 136 yd/124 m / 50 g): Silver 4911

CYCA #1 (fingering), Sandnes Garn Mandarin Petit (100% cotton, 195 yd/178 m / 50 g):
White 1001
Light Blue 5930
Navy Blue 6073
Black 1099
Pale Yellow 2002
Yellow-Orange 2515

CYCA #2 (sport/baby), Garnstudio Cotton Viscose (54% cotton, 46% rayon/viscose, 120 yd/110 m / 50 g):
Rust 06
Burgundy 07

CYCA #4 (worsted/afghan/Aran), Garnstudio Paris (100% cotton, 82 yd/75 m / 50 g): Deep Yellow 14

CYCA #3 (DK/light worsted), Garnstudio Drops Muskat (100% cotton, 109 yd/100 m / 50 g):
Turquoise 32

CYCA #2 (sport), Rauma Pavo (100% polyester, 170 yd/155 m / 50 g): Blue 2014

CYCA #0 (thread/lace), Rauma Concorde (64% rayon, 36% polyester, 137 yd/125 m / 25 g): Silver 21

All yarns/colors: 1 ball of each or leftovers

Notions: Insert pillow 15¾ in / 40 cm in diameter

Crochet Hook: U. S. E-4 / 3.5 mm

STRIPE SEQUENCE
Always hold a strand of White with a strand of Concorde Silver.
Work:
2 rnds White/Silver
2 rnds Gullfasan Silver
1 rnd Pavo Blue
1 rnd Turquoise
2 rnds Navy Blue
2 rnds Black
2 rnds White/Silver
2 rnds Pale Yellow
1 rnd Yellow-Orange
1 rnd Deep Yellow
1 rnd Rust
1 rnd Burgundy
2 rnds White/Silver
1 rnd Gullfasan Silver
1 rnd Pavo Blue
2 rnds Navy Blue

= 24 rnds and the center of the cover.
Rep the stripe sequence, working in reverse order— this means there will be 4 rnds Navy Blue at the center of the tube.

COVER
With White/Silver, ch 270 and join into a ring with 1 sl st into 1st ch.
Work around continually, omitting a sl st to join rnds. Pm at beg of rnd and move up every rnd.
Rnd 1: Ch 1, (1 sc in each of next 6 ch, 3 sc in next ch, 1 sc in each of next 6 ch, skip 2 ch) 18 times.
Rnd 2: [1 sc in each of next 6 sc, 3 sc in next sc (the center of the 3 sc of previous rnd), 1 sc in each of next 6 sc, skip 2 sc] around.
Rep Rnd 2, working in Stripe Sequence and, on the last rnd:
Rnd 48: [1 sc in each of next 6 sc, (1 sc, ch 2, 1 sc) in next sc, 1 sc in each of next 6 sc, skip 2 sc] around. Continue with White/Silver only.
Rnd 49: Sl st to 1st ch-2 ch loop, work 1 sc around each ch-2 loop, skipping all sc.
Rnd 50: Work 1 sc in each sc around.
Rnds 51-52: Work sc2tog around. Cut yarn and thread end through rem sts; tighten.
Weave in all ends neatly on WS, insert pillow and rep Rnds 49-52 on the front.

FLOWER
Flower button: With Navy Blue, ch 4 and join into a ring with 1 sl st into 1st ch. Ch 3 and work 19 dc around ring, 1 sl st in 3rd ch at beg of rnd. Cut yarn, leaving a long enough tail for sewing up.
Flower petals: With Concorde Silver, ch 4 and join into a ring with 1 sl st into 1st ch.
Rnd 1: Ch 3, 19 tr around ring, 1 sl st in 3rd ch.
Rnd 2: Ch 1, 2 sc in each tr around, 1 sl st into 1st sc.
Rnd 3: Ch 3, 2 dc in 1st sc, 3 dc in each sc around, 1 sl st into 3rd ch.
Rnd 4: (Ch 5, 1 sc in next dc) around, ending with 1 sl st into 1st ch.
Sew the flower button securely to the center of the flower and then securely attach the flower to the center on pillow front.

PINK AND TURQUOISE PILLOW

FINISHED MEASUREMENTS
15¾ in / 40 cm in diameter

MATERIALS
Yarn:
CYCA #1 (fingering), Sandnes Garn Mandarin Petit (100% cotton, 195 yd/178 m / 50 g):
Pink 4301
Clear Pink 4505
Light Yellow 2002
Aqua-mint 6803
Turquoise 6705
Apple Green 6514

CYCA #0 (thread) Sandnes Garn London (100% polyester, 164 yd/150 m / 50 g): Gold 2242

CYCA #3 (DK/light worsted) Sandnes Garn Mandarin Naturell (100% cotton, 142 yd/130 m / 50 g): Cerise 4627

CYCA #2 (sport), Rauma Pavo (100% polyester, 170 yd/155 m / 50 g): Blue 2014

CYCA #3 (DK/light worsted), Garnstudio Drops Muskat (100% cotton, 109 yd/100 m / 50 g):
Dark Plum 38
Heather 39
Dark Turquoise 32

CYCA #2 (sport/baby), Garnstudio Cotton Viscose (54% cotton, 46% rayon/viscose, 120 yd/110 m / 50 g): Rust 06

CYCA #4 (worsted/afghan/Aran), Garnstudio Paris (100% cotton, 82 yd/75 m / 50 g): Deep Yellow 14

1 tube fine silver thread

All yarns/colors: 1 ball of each or leftovers

Notions: Insert pillow 15¾ in / 40 cm in diameter

Crochet Hook: U. S. E-4 / 3.5 mm

STRIPE SEQUENCE
Always hold a strand of Pink with a strand of fine Silver thread.
Work:
3 rnds Dark Plum
2 rnds Yellow
1 rnd Heather
2 rnds Cerise
2 rnds Clear Pink
3 rnds Pink/Silver
2 rnds Apple Green
1 rnd White
2 rnds Aqua-mint
1 rnd Turquoise
1 rnd Dark Turquoise
1 rnd Blue
1 rnd Pale Yellow
1 rnd Deep Yellow
1 rnd Rust

Rep the stripe sequence, working in reverse order—this means there will be 2 rnds Rust at the center of the tube.

COVER
With Dark Plum, ch 270 and join into a ring with 1 sl st into 1st ch.
Work around continually, omitting a sl st to join rnds. Pm at beg of rnd and move up every rnd.
Rnd 1: (1 sc in each of next 3 ch, 3 sc in next ch, 1 sc in each of next 3 ch, skip 2 ch) 30 times.
Rnd 2: Work only in back loops around. [1 sc in each of next 3 sc, 3 sc in next st (the center of the 3 sc of previous rnd), 1 sc in each of next 3 sc, skip 2 sc] around.
Rep Rnd 2, working in Stripe Sequence and, on the last rnd:
Rnd 48: [1 sc in each of next 3 sc, (1 sc, ch 2, 1 sc) in next sc, 1 sc in each of next 3 sc, skip 2 sc] around. Continue with Dark Plum only.
Rnd 49: Sl st to 1st ch-2 ch loop, work 1 sc around each ch-2 loop, skipping all sc.
Rnd 50: Work 1 sc in each sc around.
Rnds 51-52: Work sc2tog around. Cut yarn and thread end through rem sts; tighten.
Weave in all ends neatly on WS, insert pillow and rep Rnds 49-52 on the front.

FLOWER
With Dark Plum, ch 4 and join into a ring with 1 sl st into 1st ch.
Rnd 1: Ch 2, 7 hdc around ring, 1 sl st into 2nd ch at beg of rnd.
Rnd 2: Ch 2 and 1 hdc in same st, 2 hdc in each hdc around, 1 sl st into 2nd ch at beg of rnd.
Rnds 3-4: Ch 1, 1 sc in each st around, 1 sl st in 1st sc.
Rnd 5: Ch 1, 2 sc in same sc, 3 sc in each sc around, 1 sl st into 1st sc.
Rnd 6: Ch 3, 2 dc in same sc, 3 dc in each sc around, 1 sl st in 3rd ch at beg of rnd.
Rnd 7: (Ch 5, 1 sc in next dc) around, 1 sl st into 1st ch. Securely attach flower to center of pillow.

Long White Vest

This vest takes a bit of time to make but is a good challenge for a beginner. And it's definitely eyecatching! If you want to try out the pattern first, start with the white scarf on page 60 before embarking on this larger piece.

LEVEL OF DIFFICULTY
Advanced

SIZES
SX/S (M/L, XL/XXL)

FINISHED MEASUREMENTS
Chest: 37¾ (42½, 52) in / 96 (108, 132) cm
Length: 48¾ (49, 50) in / 124 (125, 127) cm + 2½ in / 6 cm for flower fringe

MATERIALS
Yarn:
CYCA #1 (fingering), Dale Garn Lille Lerke (53% Merino wool, 47% cotton 155 yd/142 m / 50 g)

Yarn Color and Amounts:
Natural 0020: 700 (750, 800) g

Crochet Hook: U. S. E-4 / 3.5 mm

GAUGE
1 rep over 14 ch in Pattern A = approx. 2½ in / 6.5 cm.
Adjust hook size to obtain correct gauge if necessary.

PATTERN A (MULTIPLE OF 14 + 1 STS)

Row 1: [Ch 2, (dc2tog, ch 2, dc2tog), around next ch-5 loop, ch 2, (5 dc, ch 2, 5 dc) around next ch-2 loop] 13 (15, 19) times and end with ch 2, (dc2tog, ch2, dc2tog) around next ch-5 loop, ch 2.

Row 2: Ch 2, skip 1st ch-2 loop, (dc2tog, ch 2, 1 dc, ch 2, dc2tog) around next ch-2 loop, ch 2, skip next ch-2 loop, [(4 dc, ch 2, 4 dc) around next ch-2 loop, ch 2, skip next ch-2 loop, (dc2tog, ch 2, 1 dc, ch 2, dc2tog) around next ch-2 loop] 13 (15, 19) times; end with ch 2.

Row 3: [(Ch 2, skip 1st ch-2 loop, dc2tog around next ch-2 loop, ch 2, (1 dc, ch 2, 1 dc) in next dc, ch 2, dc2tog around next ch-2 loop, ch 2, skip next ch-2 loop, (3 dc, ch 2, 3 dc) around next ch-2 loop] 13 (15, 19) times, ending with ch 2, skip next ch-2 loop, dc2tog around nex ch-2 loop, ch 2, (1 dc, ch 2, 1 dc) in next dc, ch 2, dc2tog around next ch-2 loop, ch 2.

Row 4: Ch 2, skip ch-2 loop, dc2tog around next ch-2 loop, ch 2, (2 dc, ch 2, 2 dc) around next ch-2 loop, ch 2, dc2tog around next ch-2 loop, ch 2, skip next ch-2 loop, [(2 dc, ch 2, 2 dc) around next ch-2 loop, ch 2, skip next ch-2 loop, dc2tog around next ch-2 loop, ch 2, (2 dc, ch 2, 2 dc) around next ch-2 loop, ch 2] 13 (15, 19) times.

Row 5: Ch 1, [skip ch-2 loop, dc2tog around next ch-2 loop, ch 2, (3 dc, ch 2, 3 dc) around next ch-2 loop, ch 2, dc2tog around next ch-2 loop, ch 2, skip next ch-2 loop, 1 dc around next ch-2 loop, ch 2] 13 (15, 19) times, ending last rep with ch 1.

Row 6: Ch 1, dc2tog around ch-2 loop, ch 2, (4 dc, ch 2, 4 dc) around next ch-2 loop, ch 2, dc2tog around next ch-2 loop, [ch 2, skip ch-2 loop + 1 dc + ch-2 loop, dc2tog around next ch-2 loop, ch 2, (4 dc, ch 2, 4 dc) around next ch-2 loop, ch 2, dc2tog around next ch-2 loop] 13 (15, 19) times, ending last rep with ch 1.

Row 7: [Ch 2, (5 dc, ch 2, 5 dc) around next ch-2 loop, ch 2, skip ch-2 loop, (dc2tog, ch 2, dc2tog) around next ch-2 loop] 13 (15, 19) times, ending with ch 2, (5 dc, ch 2, 5 dc) around next ch-2 loop, ch 2.

Row 8: Ch 2, skip 1st ch-2 loop, (4 dc, ch 2, 4 dc) around next ch-2 loop, ch 2, skip next ch-2 loop, [(dc2tog, ch 2, 1 dc, ch 2, dc2tog) around next ch-2 loop, ch 2, skip next ch-2 loop, (4 dc, ch 2, 4 dc) around next ch-2 loop, ch 2] 13 (15, 19) times.

Row 9: [Ch 2, skip 1st ch-2 loop, (3 dc, ch 2, 3 dc) around next ch-2 loop, ch 2, skip next ch-2 loop, d2tog around next ch-2 loop, ch 2, (1 dc, ch 2, 1 dc) in next dc, ch 2, dc2tog around next ch-2 loop] 13 (15, 19) times, ending with ch 2, skip next ch-2 loop, (3

dc, ch 2, 3 dc) around next ch-2 loop, ch 2.

Row 10: Ch 2, skip 1st ch-2 loop, (2 dc, ch 2, 2 dc) around next ch-2 loop, ch 2, skip next ch-2 loop, [dc2tog around next ch-2 loop, ch 2, (2 dc, ch 2, 2 dc) around next ch-2 loop, ch 2, dc2tog around next ch-2 loop, ch 2, skip next ch-2 loop, (2 dc, ch 2, 2 dc) around next ch-2 loop, ch 2, skip next ch-2 loop] 13 (15, 19) times, ending with (2 dc, ch 2, 2 dc) around next ch-2 loop, ch 2.

Row 11: [Ch 2, skip 1st ch-2 loop, 1 dc around next ch-2 loop, ch 2, skip next ch-2 loop, dc2tog around next ch-2 loop, ch 2, (3 dc, ch 2, 3 dc) around next ch-2 loop, ch 2, dc2tog around next ch-2 loop] 13 (15, 19) times and end with ch 2, skip next ch-2 loop, 1 dc around next ch-2 loop, ch 2.

Row 12: Ch 2, skip ch-2 loop + 1 dc + ch-2 loop, [dc2tog around next ch-2 loop, ch 2, (4 dc, ch 2, 4 dc) around next ch-2 loop, ch 2, dc2tog around next ch-2 loop, ch 2, skip next ch-2 loop + 1 dc + ch-2 loop] 14 (16, 20) times.

Row 13: [Ch 2, (dc2tog, ch 2, dc2tog) around 1st ch-2 loop, ch 2, skip next ch-2 loop, (5 dc, ch 2, 5 dc) around next ch-2 loop] 13 (15, 19) times and end with ch 2, skip next ch-2 loop, (dc2tog, ch 2, dc2tog) around next ch-2 loop, ch 2.

Rep Rows 2-13.

PATTERN B, LOWER EDGE AND CENTER FRONT (MULTIPLE OF 14 + 9 STS)

Row 1: Ch 3 (= 1st dc), skip 3 ch, (3 dc, ch 2, 3 dc) in next ch, ch 5, skip 6 ch, 1 sc in next ch, ch 5, skip 6 ch) across, ending with (3 dc, ch 2, 3 dc) in next ch, skip 3 ch, 1 dc in last ch.

Row 2: Ch 3 (= 1st dc), [(3 dc, ch 2, 3 dc) around next ch-2 loop, ch 3, 1 sc around ch-5 loop, ch 5, 1 sc around next ch-5 loop, ch 3] across, ending with (3 dc, ch 2, 3 dc) around next ch-2 loop, 1 dc in 3rd ch at beg of previous row.

Row 3: Ch 3 (= 1st dc), [(3 dc, ch 2, 3 dc) around next ch-2 loop, ch 3, 1 sc around ch-3 loop, 6 dc around ch-5 loop, 1 sc around ch-3 loop, ch 3] across, ending with (3 dc, ch 2, 3 dc) around next ch-2 loop, 1 dc in 3rd ch at beg of previous row.

Row 4: Ch 3 (= 1st dc), [(3 dc, ch 2, 3 dc) around next ch-2 loop, (ch 1, 1 dc in next dc) 6 times, ch 1] across, ending with (3 dc, ch 2, 3 dc) around next ch-2 loop, 1 dc in 3rd ch at beg of previous row.

Row 5: Ch 3 (= 1st dc), [(3 dc, ch 2, 3 dc) around next ch-2 loop, ch 1, skip 3 dc + 1 ch + 1 dc + 1 ch, (1 bobble in next dc, ch 1) 4 times, ch 1] across. End with (3 dc, ch 2, 3 dc) around next ch-2 loop, 1 dc in

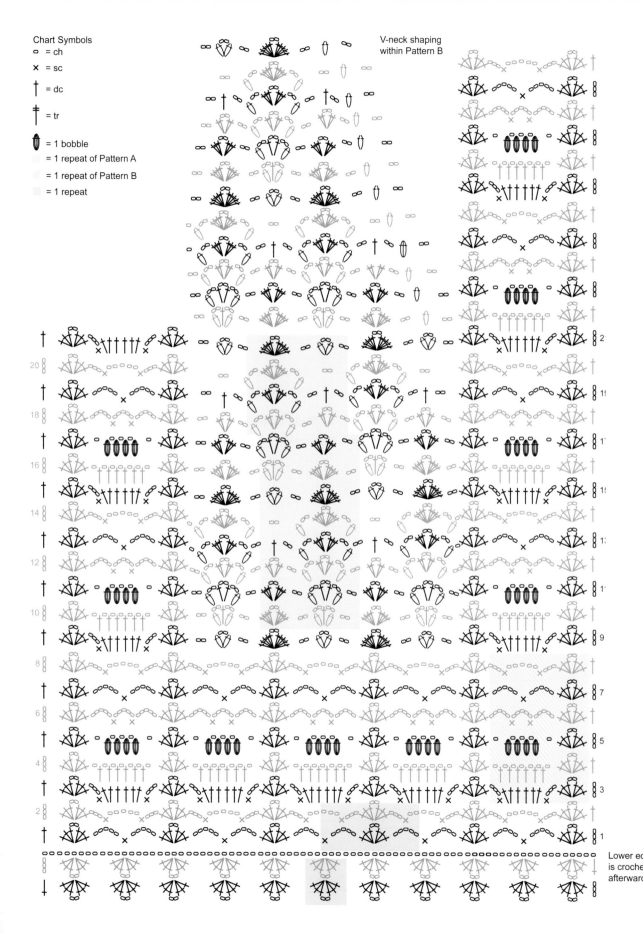

Chart Symbols

o = ch

x = sc

† = dc

‡ = tr

◍ = 1 bobble

= 1 repeat of Pattern A

= 1 repeat of Pattern B

= 1 repeat

V-neck shaping
within Pattern B

Lower edge
is crocheted
afterwards

3rd ch at beg of previous row.

Row 6: Ch 3 (= 1st dc), (3 dc, ch 2, 3 dc) around next ch loop, ch 5, skip 3 dc + 1 ch + 1 bobble, 1 sc around next ch, ch 5, skip 1 bobble + 1 ch + 1 bobble, 1 sc around next ch, ch 5] across, ending with (3 dc, ch 2, 3 dc) in next ch-2 loop, 1 dc in 3rd ch at beg of previous row.

Row 7: Ch 3 (= 1st dc), [(3 dc, ch 2, 3 dc) around next ch loop, ch 5, skip next ch-5 loop, 1 sc around next ch-5 loop, ch 5] across, ending with (3 dc, ch 2, 3 dc) around next ch-2 loop, 1 dc in 3rd ch at beg of previous row.

Rep Rows 2-7.

FRONT AND BACK

Ch 219 (247, 303) and work back and forth in Pattern B = 15 (17, 21) rep across. Work Rows 1-7 once more and then Row 2.

On the next row, work 1 rep of Pattern B, 13 (15, 19) rep of Pattern A, and 1 rep of Pattern B. The row is written out below so you can see how it is divided—it's Row 9 on the chart.

Next Row: Ch 2, (3 dc, ch 2, 3 dc) around ch-2 loop, ch 3, 1 sc around ch-3 loop, 6 dc around ch-5 loop, 1 sc around ch-3 loop, ch 3, (3 dc, ch 2, 3 dc) around next ch-2 loop = edge in Pattern B.

Continue in Pattern A. Work [ch 2, (dc2tog, ch 2, dc2tog) around next ch-5 loop, ch 2, (5 dc, ch 2, 5 dc) around next ch-2 loop] 13 (15, 19) times, ch 2, (dc2tog, ch 2, dc2tog) around next ch-5 loop, ch 2 = Pattern A.

Work Pattern B over the last rep of the row: (3 dc, ch 2, 3 dc) around ch-2 loop, ch 3, 1 sc around ch-3 loop, 6 dc around ch-5 loop, 1 sc around ch-3 loop, ch 3, (3 dc, ch 2, 3 dc) around next ch-2 loop, 1 dc in 3rd ch.

Now continue, following the chart until piece measures approx. 42½ in / 108 cm. Divide the piece for the armholes and neck shaping. The last row should be Row 21 on the chart.

LEFT FRONT

Armhole and V-neck: Work the Pattern B edge as before and then work Pattern A over the 1st 1 (2, 3) rep; turn. Work back and forth over these sts *at the same time* as decreasing for the V-neck at the right side as shown on the chart. Work until armhole depth is approx. 6¾ (7, 8) in / 17 (18, 20) cm. Now continue only over the Pattern B edge until you reach center back at back neck. Cut yarn and fasten off.

RIGHT FRONT

Work as for left front, reversing shaping to match.

BACK

Attach yarn at the side and work straight up the back in Pattern A until 2 rows rem before total length. Work over the same number of sts for shoulder as for front. Cut yarn and work opposite shoulder the same way.

FINISHING

Sew or crochet to seam shoulders. Sew or crochet the short ends of the edging and sew down along back neck.

Lower edge: Begin on WS and work in the foundation chain (see chart).

Row 1: Ch 3, [(3 dc, ch 2, 3 dc) in same ch with (3 dc, ch 2, dc 3) of Row 1, skip 6 ch, (3 dc, ch 2, 3 dc) in next st that had 1 sc] across, ending with [(3 dc, ch 2, 3 dc) in same ch with (3 dc, ch 2, dc 3) of Row 1, 1 dc in last st.

Row 2 (RS): Ch 3, [(3 dc, ch 2, 3 dc) in each ch-2 loop across, 1 dc in 3rd ch at beg of previous rnd. Cut yarn and attach at 3rd ch at beg of row. It will look best if both the 2nd and 3rd rows are worked with RS facing.

Row 3, flower edging: Ch 1, 1 sc in 3rd ch of previous row, (ch 19, 1 dc in 3rd ch from hook, ch 3, 1 sl st in same ch as dc, ch 3, 1 dc in same ch, ch 3, 1 sl st in same ch, ch 3, 1 dc in same ch, ch 3, 1 sl st in same ch, ch 7, 1 sc in 7th ch from flower, ch 8, 1 sc in next ch-2 loop) across. End with ch 19, 1 dc in 3rd ch from hook, ch 3, 1 sl st in same st as dc, ch 3, 1 dc in same ch, ch 3, 1 sl st in same ch, ch 3, 1 dc in same ch, ch 3, 1 sl st in same ch, ch 7, 1 sc in 7th ch from flower, ch 8, 1 sc in last dc.

Armhole edging: Ch 23 and work back and forth in Pattern B until edging reaches around the armhole. Don't make the strip too long or it won't fit correctly when it is sewn on. Sew or crochet the short ends together and sew or crochet the edging securely around the armhole. Attach yarn at base of armhole. Ch 1 and then work sc evenly spaced around armhole edge. Work about 2 sc around each dc / 3 ch and end with 1 sl st into 1st sc. Make sure that the stitches are evenly spaced around and the edging doesn't draw in or ruffle.

Flower edging: Ch 1, 1 sc in 1st sc, (ch 19, 1 dc in 3rd ch from hook ch 3, 1 sl st in same st as dc, ch 3, 1

dc in same ch, ch 3, 1 sl st in same ch, ch 3, 1 dc in same ch, ch 3, 1 sl st in same ch, ch 7, 1 sc in 7th ch from flower, ch 8, skip 3 sc of armhole, 1 sc in next sc) around, ending with 1 sl st into 1st sc.
Edge the other armhole the same way.

Orange Top

It's fun to have a colorful top to pull out of the closet to wear whenever you feel like drawing a little attention! The lower edge is slightly wider than the body for a more flattering silhouette.

LEVEL OF DIFFICULTY
Advanced

SIZES
S (M, L, XL)

FINISHED MEASUREMENTS
Chest: 34¾ (37¾, 41, 44) in / 88 (96, 104, 112) cm
Hip circumference: 41 (43, 45, 47) in / 104 (109, 114, 119) cm
Length: 20 (20, 20, 20) in / 51 (51, 51, 51) cm

MATERIALS
Yarn:
CYCA #1 (fingering), Dale Garn Lille Lerke (53% Merino wool, 47% cotton 155 yd/142 m / 50 g)

Lerke Yarn Colors and Amounts:
Orange 3416: 200 (250, 300, 350) g
Yellow 2215: 50 (50, 50, 50) g

CYCA #3 (DK/light worsted), Dale Garn Gullfasan (90% rayon, 10% nylon 136 yd/124 m / 50: Gold 2633: 50 (50, 50, 50) g (or leftovers)

CYCA #1 (fingering), Sandnes Garn Mandarin Petit (100% cotton, 195 yd/178 m / 50 g)

Mandarin Petit Yarn Colors and Amounts:
Pink 4301: 50 (50, 50, 50) g (or leftovers)
Light Pink 4505: 50 (50, 50, 50) g (or leftovers)
Dusty Petroleum 6822: 50 (50, 50, 50) g (or leftovers)

Crochet Hook: U. S. D-3 / 3 mm

GAUGE
1 rep over 12 ch in Pattern = approx. 1½ in / 4 cm.
1 rep in Yellow pattern = 2 in / 5 cm.
Adjust hook size to obtain correct gauge if necessary.

TECHNIQUES
Double crochet cluster (dc cl): Dc2tog in same st.
Picot: Ch 3 and 1 sl st into 1st ch.

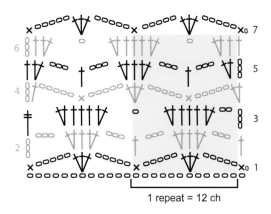

1 repeat = 12 ch

Chart Symbols

o = ch

✕ = sc

† = dc

‡ = tr

▢ = 1 repeat

PATTERN (MULTIPLE OF 12 + 1 STS)

Row 1: Begin in 2nd ch from hook, work 1 sc, (ch 5, skip 5 ch, 3 dc in next ch, ch 5, skip 5 ch, 1 sc in next ch) across.

Row 2: Ch 6 (= 1st dc + ch 3), (2 dc in 1st dc, 1 dc in next dc, 2 dc in next dc, ch 3, 1 dc in sc, ch 3) across, ending with 2 dc in 1st dc, 1 dc in next dc, 2 dc in next dc, ch 3, 1 dc in sc.

Row 3: Ch 5 (= 1st dc + ch 2), (2 dc in next dc, 1 dc in each of next 3 dc, 2 dc in next dc, ch 1) across, ending with 2 dc in next dc, 1 dc in each of next 3 dc, 2 dc in next dc, 1 tr in 3rd ch at beg of previous row.

Row 4: in Ch 3 (= 1st dc), 1 dc tr, (ch 5, skip 3 dc, 1 sc in next dc, ch 5, 3 dc around ch) across, ending with ch 5, skip 3 dc, 1 sc in next dc, ch 5, 2 dc in 3rd ch at beg of previous row.

Row 5: Ch 3 (= 1st dc), 2 dc in next dc, (ch 3, 1 dc in sc, ch 3, 2 dc in next dc, 1 dc in next dc, 2 dc in next dc) across, ending with ch 3, 1 dc in sc, ch 3, 2 dc in next dc, 1 dc in 3rd ch at beg of previous row.

Row 6: Ch 3 (= 1st dc), 1 dc in next dc, 2 dc in next dc, (ch 1, 2 dc in next dc, 1 dc in each of next 3 dc, 2 dc in next dc) across, ending with ch 1, 2 dc in next dc, 1 dc in next dc, 1 dc in 3rd ch at beg of previous row.

Row 7: Ch 1, 1 sc in 1st dc, (ch 5, 3 dc around next ch, ch 5, skip 3 dc, 1 sc in next dc) across, ending with last sc in 3rd ch at beg of previous row.
Rep Rows 2-7.

TIP

This top is rather short. If you want a longer version, just make the Orange section longer. Keep in mind that the lower section is 6¼ in / 16 cm long.

NOTE: A repeat is set between brackets [ ], or parentheses ( ), or highlighted with light blue on the chart.

The front and back pieces are worked separately and seamed. Afterwards, the edgings are crocheted around the lower edge and armholes.

BACK

With Orange, ch 133 (145, 157, 169). Work back and forth in Pattern until piece measures approx. 15½ (15½, 15½, 15½) in / 39 (39, 39, 39) cm or desired length. End with pattern Row 3 or 6 of pattern.

FRONT

Work as for back until piece measures approx. 12¾ (12¾, 12¾, 12 ¾) in / 32 (32, 32, 32) cm or desired length. End with Row 3 or 6 of pattern.
Neck shaping: Work 3 (3½, 4, 4½) rep; turn. Work back and forth over these sts until same length as back. Cut yarn and fasten off. Skip the center 5 rep and continue over the last 3 (3½, 4, 4½) rep in pattern to total length.
Sew or crochet the shoulder seams. Sew or crochet the side seams, beginning at lower edge and ending at 8 (8¼, 8¾, 9) in / 20 (21, 22, 23) cm to leave opening for armhole.

EDGING AROUND BODY

Crochet the edging around lower edge of body.

NARROW EDGING IN PINK AND GOLD (MULTIPLE OF 3 STS)

Rnd 1: Attach Light Pink at side seam with 1 sl st. Ch 1 and then work 4 sc around each ch loop and 1 sc in ch where 1 sc or 3 dc had been worked. End with 1 sl st in 1st sc.

Rnd 2: Change to Pink and adjust the stitch count on the round so it is a multiple of 3. Ch 1 and work 1 sc in each sc around. End with 1 sl st into 1st sc.

Rnd 3: Change to Gold. Ch 3, 1 dc in same st, (ch 2, skip 2 sc, 1 dc cl in next sc) around, ending with ch 2 and 1 sl st into 3rd ch at beg of rnd.

Rnd 4: Change to Pink. Ch 1, 3 sc around each ch loop around, ending with 1 sl st into 1st sc.

Rnd 5: Change to Light Pink and increase the stitch count to a multiple of 12. Ch 1 and then work 1 sc in each sc, ending with 1 sl st into 1st sc.

WIDE YELLOW BORDER (MULTIPLE OF 12 STS)

Rnd 6: Change to Yellow. (Ch 3, 1 dc, ch 3, 2 dc) in same sc, ch 4, skip 5 sc, 1 dc in next dc, ch 4, skip 5 sc, [(2 dc, ch 3, 2 dc) in next sc, ch 4, skip 5 sc, 1 dc in next dc, ch 4, skip 5 sc] around, ending with 1 sl st into 3rd ch at beg of rnd.

Rnd 7: Sl st to ch-3 loop, (ch 3, 1 dc, ch 3, 2 dc) around next ch-3 loop, ch 4, 1 dc around ch-4 loop, 1 dc in next dc, ch 4, skip 2 dc, [(2 dc, ch 3, 2 dc) around ch-3 loop, ch 4, 1 dc around ch-4 loop, 1 dc in next dc, ch 4, skip 2 dc] around, ending with 1 sl st into 3rd ch at beg of previous rnd.

Rnd 8: Sl st to ch-3 loop, (ch 3, 1 dc, ch 3, 2 dc) around ch-3 loop, ch 3, 1 dc around ch-4 loop, 1 dc in each of next 2 dc, 1 dc in ch-4 loop, ch 3, skip 2 dc, [(2 dc, ch 3, 2 dc) around ch-3 loop, ch 3, 1 dc around ch-4 loop, 1 dc in each of next 2 dc, 1 dc around ch-4 loop, ch 3, skip 2 dc] around, ending with 1 sl st into 3rd ch at beg of previous rnd.

Rnds 9-11: Sl st to ch-3 loop, (ch 3, 1 dc, ch 3, 2 dc) around ch-3 loop, ch 3, skip next ch-3 loop, 1 dc in each of next 4 dc, ch 3, skip ch-3 loop + 2 dc, [(2 dc, ch 3, 2 dc) around ch-3 loop, ch 3, skip next ch-3 loop, 1 dc in each of next 4 dc, ch 3, skip ch-3 loop + 2 dc] around, ending with 1 sl st into 3rd ch at beg of previous rnd.

Rnd 12: Sl st to ch-3 loop, (ch 3, 1 dc, ch 3, 2 dc) around ch-3 loop, ch 4, skip 2 dc + ch-3 loop + 1 dc, 1 dc in each of next 2 dc, ch 4, skip 1 dc + ch-3 loop + 2 dc, [(2 dc, ch 3, 2 dc) around ch-3 loop , ch 4, skip 2 dc + ch-3 loop + 1 dc, 1 dc in each of next 2 dc, ch 3, skip 1 dc + ch-3 loop + 2 dc] around, ending with 1 sl st into 3rd ch at beg of previous rnd.

Rnd 13: Sl st to ch-3 loop, (ch 3, 1 dc, ch 3, 2 dc) around ch-3 loop, ch 4, skip 2 dc + ch-3 loop, 1 dc between the next 2 dc, ch 4, skip 1 dc + ch-3 loop + 2 dc, [(2 dc, ch 3, 2 dc) around ch-3 loop, ch 4, skip 2 dc + ch-3 loop, 1 dc between next 2 dc, ch 3, skip 1 dc + ch-3 loop + 2 dc] around, ending with 1 sl st into 3rd ch at beg of previous rnd.

NARROW EDGING IN PINK AND GOLD (MULTIPLE OF 3 STS)

Rnds 15-19: Work as for Rnds 1-5, and, on last rnd, adjust the stitch count to a multiple of 13.

LOWER EDGE (MULTIPLE OF 13 STS),

Rnd 20: Change to Dusty Petroleum. Ch 1, (1 sc in each of the next 11 sc, ch 3, skip 2 sc) around, ending with 1 sl st into 1st sc.

Rnd 21: 1 sl st around ch-3 loop, (ch 3, 1 dc, ch 2, 1

dc-cl, ch 2, 1-dc cl) around ch 3 loop, [ch 2, skip 2 sc, 1 sc in next sc, (ch 3, skip 2 sc, 1 sc in next sc) 2 times, ch 2, (1-dc cl, ch 2, 1-dc cl, ch 2, 1-dc cl) around ch-3 loop] around, ending with ch 2, skip 2 sc, 1 sc in next sc, (ch 3, skip 2 sc, 1 sc in next sc) 2 times, ch 2, 1 sl st in 3rd ch at beg of rnd.

Rnd 22: 1 sc in 1st dc-cl, (3 sc around ch-2 loop, 1 picot, 1 sc in dc-cl, 3 sc around next ch-2 loop, 1 picot, 1 sc in dc cl, 1 sc around ch-2 loop, 2 sc around ch-3 loop, ch 3, 2 sc around next ch-3 loop, ch 3, 2 sc around next ch-3 loop, 1 sc around ch-2 loop, 1 picot, 1 sc in dc cl); end with 1 sl st into 1st sc.

FINISHING

Narrow edging around armholes:

Rnds 1-5: Attach Light Pink at center of underarm and work Narrow Edging as for body. On the 2nd rnd, adjust the stitch count to a multiple of 3.

Rnd 6: Change to Dusty Petroleum. Ch 1, 1 sc, (ch 2, skip 2 sc, 1 sc in next sc) around, ending with ch 2 and 1 sl st in 1st sc.

NECKBAND

Rnd 1: Attach Light Pink at a shoulder seam. Ch 1 and then work sc evenly spaced around neck, ending with 1 sl st into 1st sc.

Rnd 2: Change to Dusty Petroleum. Ch 1, 1 sc, (ch 2, skip 2 sc, 1 sc in next sc) around, ending with ch 2 and 1 sl st in 1st sc.

Weave in all ends neatly on WS.

Blue Top

I liked the colors for the blue coverlet shown on page 90 so much that I had to design a top with almost the same colors. This top pairs equally well with jeans or nice white pants when you want to dress up more.

LEVEL OF DIFFICULTY
Advanced

SIZES
S (M, L, XL, XXL)

FINISHED MEASUREMENTS
Chest: 39½ (43¼, 47¼, 51¼, 55¼) in / 100 (110, 120, 130, 140) cm
Length: 19¾ (19¾, 21¾, 21¾, 23¾) in / 50 (50, 55, 55, 60) cm

MATERIALS
Yarn:
CYCA #1 (fingering), Sandnes Garn Mandarin Petit (100% cotton, 195 yd/178 m / 50 g)

Yarn Colors and Amounts:
Light Blue 5930: 200 (250, 300, 350, 350) g
Denim Blue 6543: 100 (100, 100, 100, 10) g
Medium Blue 5844: 50 (50, 50, 50, 50) g
Sand 2431: 50 (50, 50, 50, 50) g (or leftovers)
White 1001: 50 (50, 50, 50, 50) g (or leftovers)

Crochet Hook: U. S. D-3 / 3 mm

GAUGE
1 rep in Pattern A over 14 ch = approx. 2 in / 5 cm.
Adjust hook size to obtain correct gauge if necessary.

TECHNIQUES
Double crochet cluster (dc cl): dc2tog in same st.
Picot: Ch 3 and then work 1 sl st into 1st ch.

Pattern A

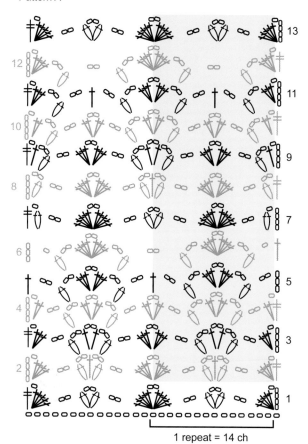

1 repeat = 14 ch

Pattern B

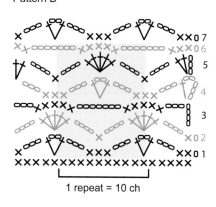

1 repeat = 10 ch

Chart Symbols

o = ch

✕ = sc

† = dc

‡ = tr

◊ = dc2tog

▢ = 1 repeat

TIP

This top is rather short, but you can lengthen the light blue section if you want. Keep in mind that the lower section measures 6 in / 15 cm.

NOTE: A repeat is set between brackets [ ], or parentheses ( ), or highlighted with light blue on the chart.

The front and back pieces are each worked separately and then seamed. The bands at the lower edge and around the armholes are worked in the round.

BACK

With Light Blue, ch 113 (127, 141, 155, 169) and work back and forth in Pattern A.

Row 1: Ch 5 (= 1st tr + ch 1), 5 dc in 1st ch, [ch 2, skip 6 ch, (dc2tog, ch 2, dc2tog) in next ch, ch 2, skip 6 ch, (5 dc, ch 2, 5 dc) in next ch] across, ending with (5 dc, ch 1, 1 tr) in last st.

Row 2: Ch 5 (= 1st tr + ch 1), 4 dc around 1st ch, [ch 2, skip next ch-2 loop, (dc2tog, ch 2, 1 dc, ch 2, dc2tog) around next ch-2 loop, ch 2, skip next ch-2 loop, (4 dc, ch 2, 4 dc) around next ch-2 loop] across, ending with ch 2, skip next ch-2 loop, (dc2tog, ch 2, 1 dc, ch 2, dc2tog) around next ch-2 loop, ch 2, skip next ch-2 loop, (4 dc, ch 1, 1 tr) in 4th ch at beg of previous row.

Row 3: Ch 5 (= 1st tr + ch 1), 3 dc around 1st ch, [ch 2, skip next ch-2 loop, dc2tog around next ch-2 loop, ch 2, (1 dc, ch 2, 1 dc) in next dc, ch 2, dc2tog around next ch-2 loop, ch 2, skip next ch-2 loop, (3 dc, ch 2, 3 dc) around next ch-2 loop] across, ending with ch 2, skip next ch-2 loop, dc2tog around next ch-2 loop, ch 2, (1 dc, ch 2, 1 dc) in next dc, ch 2, dc2tog around next ch-2 loop, ch 2, skip next ch-2 loop, (3 dc, ch 1, 1 tr) in 4th ch at beg of previous row.

Row 4: Ch 5 (= 1st tr + ch 1), 2 dc around 1st ch, [ch 2, skip next ch-2 loop, dc2tog around next ch-2 loop, ch 2, (2 dc, ch 2, 2 dc) around next ch-2 loop, ch 2, dc2tog around next ch-2 loop, ch 2, skip next ch-2 loop, (2 dc, ch 2, 2 dc) around next ch-2 loop] across, ending with ch 2, skip next ch-2 loop, dc2tog around next ch-2 loop, ch 2, (2 dc, ch 2, 2 dc) around next ch-2 loop, ch 2, dc2tog around next ch-2 loop, ch 2, skip next ch-2 loop, (2 dc, ch 1, 1 tr) in 4th ch at beg of previous row.

Row 5: Ch 5 (= 1st dc + ch 2), [skip ch-2 loop, dc2tog around next ch-2 loop, ch 2, (3 dc, ch 2, 3 dc) around next ch-2 loop, ch 2, dc2tog around next ch-2 loop, ch 2, skip next ch-2 loop, 1 dc around next ch-2 loop] across, but work the last dc in the 4th ch at beg of previous row.

Row 6: Ch 4 (= 1st dc + ch 1), skip ch-2 loop, [dc2tog around next ch-2 loop, ch 2, (4 dc, ch 2, 4 dc) around next ch-2 loop, ch 2, dc2tog around next ch-2 loop, ch 2, skip ch-2 loop + 1 dc + ch-2 loop] across, ending with dc2tog around next ch-2 loop, ch 2, (4 dc, ch 2, 4 dc) around next ch-2 loop, ch 2, dc2tog around next ch-2 loop, ch 1 and 1 dc in 3rd ch at beg of previous row.

Row 7: Ch 5 (= 1st tr + ch 1), dc2tog around next ch-1 loop, skip ch-2 loop, [(5 dc, ch 2, 5 dc) around next ch-2 loop, ch 2, skip ch-2 loop, (dc2tog, ch 2, dc2tog) around next ch-2 loop, ch 2, skip next ch-2 loop] across, ending with (5 dc, ch 2, 5 dc) around next ch-2 loop, ch 2, skip ch-2 loop, dc2tog around ch-1 loop, ch 1, 1 tr in 3rd ch at beg of previous row.

Row 8: Ch 6 (= 1st tr + ch 2), dc2tog around ch-1 loop, ch 2, skip 1st ch-2 loop, [(4 dc, ch 2, 4 dc) around next ch-2 loop, ch 2, skip next ch-2 loop, (dc2tog, ch 2, 1 dc, ch 2, dc2tog) around next ch-2 loop, ch 2, skip next ch-2 loop] across, ending with (4 dc, ch 2, 4 dc) around next ch-2 loop, ch 2, skip next ch-2 loop, dc2tog around ch-1 loop, ch 2, 1 tr in 4th ch at beg of previous row.

Row 9: Ch 5 (= 1st tr + ch 1) and 1 dc in tr, ch 2, dc2tog around ch-2 loop, ch 2, skip next ch-2 loop, [(3 dc, ch 2, 3 dc) around next ch-2 loop, ch 2, skip next ch-2 loop, dc2tog around next ch-2 loop, ch 2, (1 dc, ch 2, 1 dc) in next dc, ch 2, dc2tog around next ch-2 loop, ch 2, skip next ch-2 loop] across, ending with (3 dc, ch 2, 3 dc) around next ch-2 loop, ch 2, skip next ch-2 loop, dc2tog around next ch-2 loop, ch 2, (1 dc, ch 1, 1 tr) in 4th ch at beg of previous row.

Row 10: Ch 5 (= 1st tr + ch 1), 2 dc around ch-1 loop, ch 2, dc2tog round next ch-2 loop, ch 2, skip next ch-2 loop, [(2 dc, ch 2, 2 dc) around next ch-2 loop, ch 2, skip next ch-2 loop, dc2tog around next ch-2 loop, ch 2, (2 dc, ch 2, 2 dc) around next ch-2 loop, ch 2, dc2tog around next ch-2 loop, ch 2, skip next ch-2

loop] across, ending with (2 dc, ch 2, 2 dc) around next ch-2 loop, ch 2, skip next ch-2 loop, dc2tog around next ch-2 loop, ch 2, (2 dc, ch 1, 1 tr) in 4th ch at beg of previous row.

Row 11: Ch 5 (= 1st tr + ch 1), 3 dc around ch-1 loop, ch 2, dc2tog around next ch-2 loop, ch 2, skip next ch-2 loop, [1 dc around next ch-2 loop, ch 2, skip next ch-2 loop, dc2tog around next ch-2 loop, ch 2, (3 dc, ch 2, 3 dc) around next ch 2 loop, ch 2, dc2tog around next ch-2 loop, ch 2, skip next ch-2 loop] across, ending with 1 dc around next ch-2 loop, ch 2, skip next ch-2 loop, dc2tog around next ch-2 loop, ch 2, 3 dc around ch-1 loop, ch 1, 1 tr in 4th ch at beg of previous row.

Row 12: Ch 5 (= 1st tr + ch 1), 4 dc around ch-1 loop, ch 2, [dc2tog around ch-2 loop, ch 2, skip ch-2 loop + 1 dc + ch-2 loop, dc2tog around next ch-2 loop, ch 2, (4 dc, ch 2, 4 dc) around next ch-2 loop, ch 2] across, ending with dc2tog around next ch-2 loop, ch 2, skip ch-2 loop + 1 dc + ch-2 loop, dc2tog around next ch-2 loop, ch 2, 4 dc around ch-1 loop, ch 1, 1 tr in 4th ch at beg of previous row.

Row 13: Ch 5 (= 1st tr + ch 1), 5 dc around ch-1 loop, [ch 2, skip next ch-2 loop, (dc2tog, ch 2, dc2tog) around next ch-2 loop, ch 2, skip next ch-2 loop, (5 dc, ch 2, 5 dc) around next ch-2 loop] across, ending with ch 2, skip next ch-2 loop, (dc2tog, ch 2, dc2tog) around next ch-2 loop, ch 2, skip next ch-2 loop, (5 dc around ch-1 loop, ch 1, 1 tr in 4th ch at beg of previous row.

Rep Rows 2-13 until piece measures approx. 13¾ (13¾, 15 ¾, 15 ¾, 17¾) in / 35 (35, 40, 40, 45) cm or desired length.

FRONT

Work as for back until piece measures approx. 10¾ (10¾, 12¾, 12¾, 14½) in / 27 (27, 32, 32, 37) cm.

Neck: Work 2½ (3, 3½, 4, 4) rep in pattern and turn. Work back and forth over these sts until same total length as back. Cut yarn and fasten off. Skip the center 3 (3, 3, 3, 4) rep. Attach yarn and work to same total length over the last 2½ (3, 3½, 4, 4) rep at the left side. Cut yarn and fasten off. Sew or crochet shoulder seams. Sew or crochet side seams, beginning at lower edge and up approx. 8 (8¼, 8¾, 9, 9½) in / 20 (21, 22, 23, 24) cm; leave rest open for armholes.

EDGING AROUND BODY
NARROW PANEL IN WHITE, SAND, AND MEDIUM BLUE
(MULTIPLE OF 3 STS)
Rnd 1: Attach Sand at a side seam with 1 sl st. Ch 1 and then work 4 sc over each ch loop and 1 sc in each ch where you had worked 1 sc or 3 dc; end with 1 sl st into 1st sc.

Rnd 2: Change to White and adjust stitch count to a multiple of 3. Ch 1 and work 1 sc in each sc around, ending with 1 sl st into 1st sc.

Rnd 3: Change to Medium Blue. Ch 3, 1 dc in same st, (ch 2, skip 2 sc, dc2tog in next sc) around ending with ch 2 and 1 sl st into 3rd ch at beg of rnd.

Rnd 4: Change to White. Ch 1, 3 sc around each ch loop around; end with 1 sl st into 1st sc.

Rnd 5: Change to Sand. Increase evenly spaced around to obtain a stitch count that is a multiple of 10. Ch 1, 1 sc in each sc; end with 1 sl st into 1st sc.

WIDE DENIM PANEL (MULTIPLE OF 10 STS)
Rnds 6-15: Change to Denim Blue and work Pattern B.

Rnd 16: Ch 1, 1 sc in 1st sc, and 1 sc in next sc, [(ch 3, skip 3 sc, (1 dc, ch 2, 1 dc) in same sc, ch 3, skip 3 sc, 1 sc in each of next 3 sc] around, ending with 1 sc in last sc and 1 sl st in 1st sc.

Rnd 17: Ch 1, 1 sc in 1st sc, [ch 4, 5 dc around ch-2 loop, ch 4, skip 1 sc, 1 sc in next sc (the center of the 3)] around, ending with ch 4, 5 dc around ch-2 loop, ch 4, 1 sl st in 1st sc.

Rnd 18: Ch 7 (= 1st tr + ch 3), (1 sc in each of next 5 dc, ch 7) around, ending with 1 sc in each of next 5 dc, ch 3, and 1 sl st in 4th ch at beg of rnd.

Rnd 19: Ch 5 (=1st dc + ch 2) and 1 dc in same st, [ch 3, skip 1 sc, 1 sc in each of next 3 sc, ch 3, skip 1 sc +3 ch, (1 dc, ch 2, 1 dc) in next ch] around, ending with ch 3, skip 1 sc, 1 sc in each of next 3 sc, ch 3, 1 sl st in 3rd ch at beg of rnd.

Rnd 20: Ch 3 (= 1st dc) 2 dc around ch-2 loop, [ch 4, skip 1 sc, 1 sc in next sc (the center sc of the 3), ch 4, 5 dc around next ch-2 loop] around, ending with ch 4, skip 1 sc, 1 sc in next sc, ch 4, 2 dc in 1st ch-2 loop of rnd, 1 sl st into 3rd ch at beg of rnd.

Rnd 21: Ch 1, 1 sc in 3rd ch of previous rnd, 1 sc in each of next 2 dc, (ch 7, 1 sc in each of next 5 dc) around, ending with ch 7, 1 sc in each of last 2 dc, 1 sl st into 1st sc.

Rnd 22: Ch 1, 1 sc in 1st sc, 1 sc in next sc, [ch 3, skip 1 sc + 3 ch, (1 dc, ch 2, 1 dc) in next ch, ch 3, skip 1 sc, 1 sc in each of next 3 sc] around, ending with 1 sc in each of last 2 sc, 1 sl st into 1st sc.
Rep Rnds 7-9.

NARROW PANEL IN WHITE, SAND, AND MEDIUM BLUE (MULTIPLE OF 3 STS)
The stitch count automatically increased since the previous time you worked this panel.

Rnds 23-27: Work as for Rnds 1-5 but, on the last rnd, adjust the stitch count for a multiple of 13.

BOTTOM PANEL (MULTIPLE OF 13 STS)
Rnd 28: Change to Medium Blue. Ch 1, (1 sc in each of next 11 sc, ch 3, skip 2 sc) around; end with 1 sl st into 1st sc.

Rnd 29: 1 sl st around ch-3 loop, (ch 3, 1 dc, ch 2, dc2tog, ch 2, dc2tog) around ch-3 loop, [ch 2, skip 2 sc, 1 sc in next sc, (ch 3, skip 2 sc, 1 sc in next sc) 2 times, ch 2 (dc2tog, ch 2, dc2tog, ch 2, dc2tog) around ch-3 loop] around, ending with ch 2, skip 2 sc, 1 sc in next sc, (ch 3, skip 2 sc, 1 sc in next sc) 2 times, ch 2, 1 sl st in 3rd ch at beg of rnd.

Rnd 30: 1 sc in 1st dc cl, (3 sc around ch-2 loop, 1 picot, 1 sc in dc cl, 3 sc around next ch-2 loop, 1 picot, 1 sc in dc cl, 1 sc around ch-2 loop, 2 sc around ch-3 loop, ch 3, 2 sc around next ch-3 loop, 1 sc around ch-2 loop, 1 picot, 1 sc in dc cl) around, ending with 1 sl st into 1st sc.

FINISHING
Narrow edging around armholes: Attach Sand at center of underarm and work Narrow Panel as for Body. On Rnd 2, adjust stitch count to a multiple of 3.

Neckband:
Rnd 1: Attach Light Blue at a shoulder seam.
Ch 1 and then work in sc evenly spaced around; end with 1 sl st into 1st sc.

Rnd 2: Change to White. Ch 1 and work 1 sc in each sc around; end with 1 sl st into 1st sc.

Rnd 3: Change to Sand. Work as for Rnd 2.
Weave in all ends neatly on WS.

Bikini

I crocheted a colorful bikini with leftover yarns. Shocking pink and bright colors are so pretty against a nice tan! But the set can be equally pretty in white, yellow, and beige, for example, and in an entirely different way. You can adjust the sizing as you like. Begin with 9 fewer or more sts to subtract or add 1 inch / 2.5 cm to the given measurements. Just keep in mind that the fabric is quite elastic, so don't make the set too big.

LEVEL OF DIFFICULTY
Intermediate

SIZES
XS (S/M, L/XL)

FINISHED MEASUREMENTS
SHORTS
Hip circumference: approx. 30 (33, 36) in / 76 (84, 91) cm
Total length as measured at the side: 9¾ (10¼, 10¾) in / 25 (26, 27) cm

TOP
Width at lower edge of a triangle: approx. 8 (8¾, 9¾) in/ 20 (22.5, 25) cm
Length: approx. 8 (8¼, 8¾) in / 20 (21, 22) cm

MATERIALS
Yarn:
You need 100 g of Cerise and leftover amounts of all the other colors.

CYCA #2 (sport/baby), Garnstudio Cotton Viscose (54% cotton, 46% rayon/viscose, 120 yd/110 m / 50 g): Cerise 08 and Bordeaux 07

CYCA #3 (DK/light worsted), Garnstudio Drops Muskat (100% cotton, 109 yd/100 m / 50 g): Dark Plum 38

CYCA #1 (fingering), Rauma PT Pandora (100% cotton, 197 yd/180 m / 50 g): Crab Apple Green 215

CYCA #1 (fingering), Sandnes Garn Mandarin Petit (100% cotton, 195 yd/178 m / 50 g):
Dark Orange 2709
White 1002
Light Yellow 2002
Orange 2515
Turquoise 6705
Aqua-mint 6803
Pink 4301
Shocking Pink 4505

CYCA #0 (thread) Sandnes Garn London (100% polyester, 164 yd/150 m / 50 g):
Gold 2242, work with yarn doubled

Notions: 1 button

Crochet Hook: U. S. size D-3 / 3 mm

GAUGE
1 rep in Pattern over 9 ch = approx. 1 in / 2.5 cm.
Adjust hook size to obtain correct gauge if necessary.

PATTERN WORKED BACK AND FORTH (MULTIPLE OF 9 + 3 STS)

Row 1: Beg in 2nd ch from hook, work 2 sc in 1st ch, (1 sc in each of next 3 ch, 3 sc in next ch, 1 sc in each of next 3 ch, skip 2 ch) across, ending with 1 sc in each of next 3 ch and 2 sc in last ch.

Row 2: Work through back loops only on RS and front loops only on WS.

Ch 1, 2 sc in 1st sc, [1 sc in each of next 3 sc, 3 sc in next sc (the center of the 3 sc of previous row), 1 sc in each of next 3 sc, skip 2 sc] across, ending with 1 sc in next 3 sc and 2 sc in last sc.

Rep Row 2 throughout while also working in Stripe Sequence.

PATTERN WORKED IN THE ROUND (MULTIPLE OF 9 STS)

Rnd 1: Ch 1, 2 sc in 1st ch, (1 sc in each of next 3 ch, 3 sc in next ch, 1 sc in each of next 3 ch, skip 2 ch) around, ending with 1 sc in each of next 3 ch and 1 sc in same ch where the 1st 2 sc were worked, 1 sl st into 1st sc.

Rnd 2: Work through back loops only. Ch 1, 2 sc in 1st sc, [1 sc in each of next 3 sc, 3 sc in next sc (the center of the 3 sc of previous row), 1 sc in each of next 3 sc, skip 2 sc] around, ending with 1 sc in each of next 3 sc and 1 sc in same ch where the 1st 2 sc were worked, 1 sl st into 1st sc.

Rep Rnd 2 throughout while also working in Stripe Sequence.

STRIPE SEQUENCE

Begin the new color from the right side of the top each time.

2 rows/rnds Bordeaux
2 rows/rnds Dark Orange
1 row/rnd Orange
1 row/rnd Light Yellow
1 row/rnd Gold, doubled yarn
2 rows/rnds Turquoise
2 rows/rnds Aqua-mint
1 row/rnd White
1 row/rnd Crab Apple Green
2 rows/rnds Pink
2 rows/rnds Shocking Pink
1 row/rnd Cerise
1 row/rnd Dark Plum
1 row/rnd Yellow

TOP

With Bordeaux, ch 63 (72, 81) and work back and forth in Pattern and Stripe Sequence. When piece measures 2 (2½, 2¾) in / 5 (6, 7) cm, decrease 1 st at each side on every other row until 3 sts rem. When decreasing, check to make sure the pattern stitch count is correct. Cut yarn and fasten off.

Make a second piece the same way.

Edging around the triangle: Attach Cerise at lower right edge, with RS facing.

Rnd 1: Ch 6 (= 1st dc + ch 3), 1 sc around ch-2 loop of foundation chain, (ch 3, 1 sc around next ch-2 loop) along lower edge; end with ch 3 and 1 dc in last st. Continue in sc up along the side, working 3 sc in the tip and then down the next side; end with 1 sl st in 3rd ch at beg of rnd.

Rnd 2: Ch 1, 1 sc in 1st st (2 sc in ch-3 loop, 1 sc in next sc) around lower edge and then 3 sc in dc at the of edging. Work sc evenly spaced up side, 3 sc in tip and sc evenly spaced along opposite side. End with 2 sc in same dc as 1st sc of rnd and 1 sl st in 1st sc. The edging should be somewhat tight, so that the cup bows out a little.

Rnd 3: Ch 1 and then work sc in each sc to the corner, 3 sc in corner st, 1 sc in each sc up side to tip. Now crochet a cord—ch 48 (52, 56); turn and, beg in 2nd ch from hook, work 1 sc in each ch, continue along the left side of triangle with 1 sc in each sc, ending with 2 sc in same sc as 1st sc of rnd and then 1 sl st into 1st sc. Rep around the other triangle.

Cord: With Cerise, make a chain 47¼ (51¼, 55¼) in / 120 (130, 140) cm long or the length you need so the cord goes around your chest + enough to tie a bow. Beg in 2nd ch from hook, work 1 sc in each ch. Draw the cord through the holes at lower part of each triangle.

SHORTS

With Bordeaux, ch 279 (306, 333). Rnd begins at center back. Pm and move up marker at beg of rnd. Work in Pattern in the round and Stripe Sequence until piece measures 6 (6¼, 6¾) in / 15 (16, 17) cm. If you want to shorten or lengthen the shorts, make the adjustment at this point.

Increases at center back: Increase 1 st at each side of marker on every other rnd a total of 4 times. Work new sts only in sc. Piece now measures approx. 8 (8¼, 8¾) in / 20 (21, 22) cm.

Divide for the legs: Work 1 sc in each of the 1st 5 sc of the rnd; turn and work back over 10 sc (= 5 sts on each side of marker at center back). These 10 sts will be used for a gusset. Work back and forth in sc over these sts for 2 (2, 2¾) in / 5 (5, 7) cm. Cut yarn and fasten off. Sew the gusset edge to edge to the 10 centermost sts at center front. Now work the legs in the round.

Right leg: Begin at the back where the gusset ends. Work in pattern as before, but, when you come to the gusset, continue in pattern and work 2 (2, 3) rep along the gusset. Begin the next rnd at the center of gusset (inside of the leg). Continue as est until leg measures approx. 1½ in / 4 cm or desired length.

Left leg: Work as for right leg.

FINISHING

Waist: Attach Cerise in 1st ch-2 loop at beg of rnd with 1 sl st and then work back and forth.

Row 1: Ch 1, 1 sc around ch-2 loop, (ch 4, 1 sc around next ch-2 loop) across; end with 1 sc around same ch-2 loop as 1st sc of row and then ch 7. The 7 ch sts will surround a buttonhole.

Row 2: Beginning in 2nd ch from hook, work 1 sc in each of next 6 ch, (1 sc in sc, 4 sc around ch-4 loop) across; end with 1 sc in last sc.

Row 3: Ch 1 and then work 1 sc in each sc until 5 sc rem, ch 2, skip 2 sc for buttonhole, 1 sc in each of the last sc of row.

Row 4: Ch 1 and work 1 sc in each sc across, with 2 sc around ch-2 loop.

Cord: With Cerise, make a cord 51¼ (55¼, 59) in / 130 (140, 150) cm long; turn. Beg in 2nd ch from hook, work 1 sc in each ch across.

Beginning at center front, thread the cord through the row of roles at the top of the shorts.

Sew a button centered across from buttonhole.

Pink Shawl

Pink is so pretty against a nice tan. It's always a good idea to have a shawl on hand in the summertime, in case it suddenly cools off. This shawl can be tied around your hips when you are wearing your bikini on the beach.

LEVEL OF DIFFICULTY
Intermediate

FINISHED MEASUREMENTS
Width at top: approx. 72½ in / 184 cm
Length down center back: approx. 45¼ in / 115 cm excluding fringe

MATERIALS
Yarn:
CYCA #2 (sport/baby), Garnstudio Cotton Viscose (54% cotton, 46% rayon/viscose, 120 yd/110 m / 50 g), Cerise 08: 350 g

Alternate Yarn Suggestions:
CYCA #3 (DK/light worsted), Sandnes Garn Mandarin Medi (100% cotton, 147 yd/134 m / 50 g)
CYCA #3 (DK/light worsted), Rauma Garn Petunia (100% cotton, 120 yd/110 m / 50 g)

Crochet Hook: U. S. size D-3 / 3 mm

TECHNIQUES

Dc3tog over 3 sts with an extra yarnover: Yarn around hook twice, insert hook into 1st dc and bring yarn through dc, yarn around hook and through 2 loops = 2 loops on hook; (yarn around hook, insert into next dc and bring yarn through dc, yarn around hook and through 2 loops) 2 times = 5 loops on hook. Yarn around hook and through 4 loops, yarn around hook and through the last 2 loops.

Double crochet cluster (dc cl): dc3tog over 3 sts with an extra yarnover.

Ch 3.

Row 1: Work (2 dc, ch 2, 3 dc, ch 4, 3 dc, ch 2, 3 dc) in 1st ch.

Row 2: Ch 3, (3 dc, ch 2, 3 dc) around ch-2 loop, ch 3, 5 dc around ch-4 loop, ch 3, (3 dc, ch 2, 3 dc) around ch-2 loop.

Row 3: Ch 3, (3 dc, ch 2, 3 dc) around ch-2 loop, ch 3, 2 dc in 1st dc, 1 dc in each of next 3 dc, 2 dc in next dc, ch 3, (3 dc, ch 2, 3 dc) around ch-2 loop.

Row 4: Ch 3, (3 dc, ch 2, 3 dc) around ch-2 loop, ch 4, 1 dc in each of next 3 dc, 2 dc in next dc, 1 dc in each of next 3 dc, ch 4, (3 dc, ch 2, 3 dc) around ch-2 loop.

Row 5: Ch 3, (3 dc, ch 2, 3 dc) around ch-2 loop, ch 4, 1 dc in 1st dc, (ch 1, 1 dc in next dc) 7 times, ch 4, (3 dc, ch 2, 3 dc) around ch-2 loop.

Row 6: Ch 3, (3 dc, ch 2, 3 dc) around ch-2 loop, ch 5, 1 dc in 1st dc, (ch 2, 1 dc in next dc) 7 times, ch 5, (3 dc, ch 2, 3 dc) around ch-2 loop.

Row 7: Ch 3, (3 dc, ch 2, 3 dc) around ch-2 loop, ch 6, (3 dc around next ch-2 loop) 7 times, ch 6, (3 dc, ch 2, 3 dc) around ch-2 loop.

Row 8: Ch 3, (3 dc, ch 2, 3 dc) around ch-2 loop, ch 7, (dc3tog with extra yarnover over next 3 dc, ch 4) 6 times, dc3tog with extra yarnover over next 3 dc, ch 7, (3 dc, ch 2, 3 dc) around ch-2 loop.

Row 9: Ch 3, (3 dc, ch 2, 3 dc) around ch-2 loop, ch 3, skip 3 ch, 5 dc in next ch, ch 3, skip 3 ch + 1 dc cl, 1 sc around ch-4 loop, (ch 4, 1 sc around next ch-4 loop) 5 times, ch 3, skip 3 ch, 5 dc in next ch, ch 3, (3 dc, ch 2, 3 dc) around ch-2 loop.

Row 10: Ch 3, (3 dc, ch 2, 3 dc) around ch-2 loop, ch 3, 2 dc in 1st dc, 1 dc in each of next 3 dc, 2 dc in next dc, ch 3, 1 sc around ch-4 loop, (ch 4, 1 sc around next ch-4 loop) 4 times, ch 3, 2 dc in 1st dc, 1 dc in each of next 3 dc, 2 dc in next dc, ch 3, (3 dc, ch 2, 3 dc) around ch-2 loop.

Row 11: Ch 3, (3 dc, ch 2, 3 dc) around ch-2 loop, ch 4, 1 dc in each of 1st 3 dc, 2 dc in next dc, 1 dc in each of next 3 dc, ch 4, 1 sc around ch-4 loop, (ch 4, 1 sc around next ch-4 loop) 3 times, ch 4, 1 dc in each of 1st 3 dc, 2 dc in next dc, 1 dc in each of next 3 dc, ch 4, (3 dc, ch 2, 3 dc) around ch-2 loop.

Row 12: Ch 3, (3 dc, ch 2, 3 dc) around ch-2 loop, ch 4, 1 dc in 1st dc, (ch 1, 1 dc in next dc) 7 times, ch 4, 1 sc around ch-4 loop, (ch 4, 1 sc around next ch-4 loop) 2 times, ch 4, 1 dc in 1st dc, (ch 1, 1 dc in next dc) 7 times, ch 4, (3 dc, ch 2, 3 dc) around ch-2 loop.

Row 13: Ch 3, (3 dc, ch 2, 3 dc) around ch-2 loop, ch 5, 1 dc in 1st dc, (ch 2, 1 dc in next dc) 7 times, ch 5, 1 sc around ch-4 loop, ch 4, 1 sc around next ch-4 loop, ch 5, 1 dc in 1st dc, (ch 2, 1 dc in next dc) 7 times, ch 5, (3 dc, ch 2, 3 dc) around ch-2 loop.

Row 14: Ch 3, (3 dc, ch 2, 3 dc) around ch-2 loop, ch 6, (3 dc around next ch-2 loop) 7 times, 1 sc around ch-4 loop, ch 6, (3 dc around next ch-2 loop) 7 times, ch 6, (3 dc, ch 2, 3 dc) around ch-2 loop.

Row 15: Ch 3, (3 dc, ch 2, 3 dc) around ch-2 loop, ch 7, (dc3tog over next 3 dc, ch 4) 6 times, dc3tog over next 3 dc, ch 7, (dc3tog over next 3 dc, ch 4) 6 times, dc3tog over next 3 dc, ch 7, (3 dc, ch 2, 3 dc) around ch-2 loop.

Rep Rows 9-15 until shawl measures approx. 45¼ in / 115 cm down center back. Do *not* cut yarn.

Edging with flower fringe: Work 1 row sc along the top edge of shawl, with 4 sc around each ch-4 loop and 6 sc around each ch-7 loop. Now work down the diagonal edge as follows: Work 3 sc in corner and 1 sc around 1st ch-3 loop along the side, (ch 19, 1 dc in 3rd ch from hook, ch 3, 1 sl st in same st as dc, ch 3, 1 dc in same ch, ch 3, 1 sl st in same ch, ch 3, 1 dc in same ch, ch 3, 1 sl st in same ch, ch 7, 1 sc in 7th ch from flower, ch 8, 1 sc around next ch-3 loop) rep along the diagonal sides, but, at the tip, do not skip the next ch-3 loop; instead, work 1 sc and a flower fringe in the tip before you work around the next ch-3 loop. Work 1 row sc along top edge.

Beige Pillow, Candle Holder Cover and Cup Cozy

What about making a few small items to sample the same pattern as for the pink cardigan on page 42, or the silver-blue pillow on page 40?

LEVEL OF DIFFICULTY
Intermediate

FINISHED MEASUREMENTS
Pillow: 19¾ x 19¾ in / 50 x 50 cm

CUP COZY
Circumference: approx. 8 in / 20 cm
Height: approx. 4¾ in / 12 cm

CANDLE HOLDER COVER
Circumference: approx. 11 in / 28 cm
Height: approx. 6 in / 15 cm
This cover will fit over a standard jam jar.

MATERIALS
Yarn:
CYCA #3 (DK/light worsted), Rauma Garn Mitu (50% wool, 50% alpaca, 109 yd/100 m / 50 g): Beige SFN73, 400 g for the pillow, 50 g or leftover yarn for the candle cover and cup cozy

Notions: Insert pillow, 19¾ x 19¾ in / 50 x 50 cm

Crochet Hook: U. S. size G-6 / 4 mm

GAUGE
1 rep over 10 ch in Pattern A = 2½ in / 6 cm.
Adjust hook size to obtain correct gauge if necessary.

Pattern B

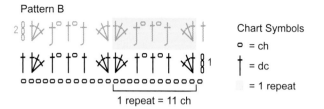

Chart Symbols

○ = ch

† = dc

▢ = 1 repeat

1 repeat = 11 ch

TECHNIQUES

Front post double crochet (FPdc): This is a double crochet stitch that is worked around the post of a dc in the previous round. Yarn around hook. Beg on RS, insert hook on the right side of the dc, push hook around to left side of st and to front; catch yarn. With WS facing, the hook goes in from the back, on right side of dc, around the dc, and to the front on left side; catch yarn. Complete stitch as for regular double crochet.

Half-double crochet cluster (hdc cl): 3 hdc crocheted together into the same st. (Yarn around hook, insert hook into st and catch yarn) 3 times; yarn around hook and through all loops on hook.

PATTERN A (MULTIPLE OF 10 + 1 STS)

The chart for Pattern A is the same as the pattern chart on page 44.

Row 1: Ch 3 (= 1st hdc + ch 1), 1 dc in each of the next 3 ch. [ch 2, skip 2 ch, 1 sc in next ch, ch 2, skip 2 ch, 1 dc in each of next 2 ch, (1 dc, ch 2, 1 dc) in next ch, 1 dc in each of next 2 ch] across, ending with ch 1 and 2 hdc in last ch.

Row 2: Ch 1, 1 sc in hdc, ch 2, (1 FPdc around each of the next 3 dc, ch 2, 1 FPdc around each of the next 3 dc, ch 2, 1 sc around ch-2 loop, ch 2) across, ending with 1 FPdc around each of the next 3 dc, ch 2, 1 FPdc around each of the next 3 dc, ch 2, 1 sc in 2nd ch at beg of previous row.

Row 3: Ch 3 (= 1st hdc + ch 1), 3-hdc cl in the 1st sc, ch 1, [1 FPdc around each of the next 6 dc, ch 1, (3-hdc cl, ch 2, 3-hdc cl) in sc, ch 1] across, ending with 1 FPdc around each of the next 6 dc, ch 1, (3-hdc cl, ch 1, 3-hdc cl) in last sc.

Rows 4-6: Ch 3 (= 1st hdc + ch 1), skip 1 ch + 1 hdc-cl, 3 hdc around next ch loop, ch 1, [1 FPdc around each of the next 6 dc, ch 1, (3-hdc cl, ch 2, 3-hdc cl), around next ch-2 loop, ch 1] across, ending with 1 FPdc around each of the next 6 dc, ch 1, 3-hdc cl around next ch, ch 1, 1 hdc in 2nd ch at beg of previous row.

Row 7: Ch 1, 1 sc in hdc, ch 2, (1 FPdc around each of the next 3 dc, ch 2, 1 FPdc around each of the next 3 dc, ch 2, 1 sc around ch-2 loop, ch 2) across, ending with 1 FPdc around each of the next 3 dc, ch 2, 1 FPdc around each of the next 3 dc, ch 2, 1 sc in 2nd ch at beg of previous row.

Row 8: Ch 3 (= 1st hdc + ch 1), (1 FPdc around each of the next 3 dc, ch 2, 1 sc around ch-2 loop, ch 2, 1 FPdc around each of the next 3 dc, ch 2) across, ending with 1 FPdc around each of the next 3 dc, ch 2, 1 sc around ch-2 loop, ch 2, 1 FPdc around each of the next 3 dc, ch 1, 1 hdc in last sc.

Row 9: Ch 2 (= 1st hdc), 1 FPdc around each of the next 3 dc, [ch 1, (3-hdc cl, ch 2, 3-hdc cl) in next sc, ch 1, 1 FPdc around each of the next 6 dc] across, ending with ch 1, (3-hdc cl, ch 2, 3-hdc cl) in next sc, ch 1, 1 FPdc around each of the next 3 dc, 1 hdc in 2nd ch at beg of previous row.

Rows 10-12: Ch 2 (= 1st hdc), 1 FPdc around each of the next 3 dc, [ch 1, (3-hdc cl, ch 2, 3-hdc cl) around ch-2 loop, ch 1, 1 FPdc around each of the next 6 dc] across, ending with ch 1, (3-hdc cl, ch 2, 3-hdc cl) in next ch-2 loop, ch 1, 1 FPdc in each of the next 3 dc, 1 hdc in 2nd ch at beg of previous row.

Row 13: Ch 2 (= 1st hdc), (1 FPdc around each of next 3 dc, ch 2, 1 sc around ch-2 loop, ch 2, 1 FPdc around each of the next 3 dc, ch 2) across, ending with 1 FPdc around each of the next 3 dc, ch 1, 1 hdc in 2nd ch at beg of previous row.

PATTERN B (MULTIPLE OF 11+ 1 STS)

Row 1: Beg in 3rd ch from hook, work 3 dc in next ch, [skip 2 ch, (1 dc in next ch, ch 1, skip 1 ch) 2 times, 1 dc in next ch, skip 2 ch, (3 dc in next ch) 2 times] across, ending with skip 2 ch, 1 dc in next ch, ch 1, skip 1 ch) 2 times, 1 dc in next ch, skip 2 ch, 3 dc in next ch, 1 dc in last ch.

Row 2: Ch 3 (= 1st dc), [3 dc in next dc, skip 2 dc, 1 FPdc around next dc, ch 1, 1 dc in next dc, ch 1, 1 FPdc around next dc, skip 2 dc, 3 dc in next dc] across, ending with 1 dc in 3rd ch at beg of previous row.

Rep Row 2.

BEIGE PILLOW

FRONT
Ch 62 and work back and forth in Pattern A until piece measures approx. 19¾ in / 50 cm. It will look best if you end with either Row 7 or 13 of pattern.

BACK
Ch 61.
Row 1: Beg in 3rd ch from hook, work 1 dc in each ch = 58 dc.
Row 2: Ch 3 (= 1st dc) and work 1 dc in each dc, with the last dc in the 3rd ch at beg of previous row.
Rep Row 2 until piece measures 19¾ in / 50 cm.

FINISHING
Place the pieces with WS facing WS.
Rnd 1: Join the back and front with sc evenly spaced along 3 sides, and 3 sc in each corner st. On the 4th side, work sc only on the front. End with 1 sl st into 1st sc.
Rnd 2: Work hdc3tog in each corner st and, otherwise, work: Ch 2 (= 1st hdc), hdc2tog, ch 1, skip 1 sc, (hdc3tog in the next st, ch 1, skip 1 sc) around, ending with 1 sl st into 1st hdc.
Rnd 3: Ch 1, (1 sc in hdc cl, 1 sc around ch) along each side and, at corners, work 3 sc around ch on each side of hdc cl. End with 1 sl st into 1st sc.
Rnd 4: Ch 1 and then work 1 crab st (= sc worked from left to right) in each sc. Insert pillow and seam opening.

CUP COZY AND CANDLE HOLDER COVER

NOTE: Work Pattern A or B back and forth and then seam sides. The numbers outside parentheses are for the cup cozy and numbers within parentheses are for the candle holder cover.

Ch 31 (41) for Pattern A and 34 (45) for Pattern B. Work in pattern until piece measures 3¼ (5¼) in / 8 (13) cm. Seam short ends.

Edging
Rnd 1: Attach yarn at seam and work 1 sc in each st, adjusting stitch count to 32 (44) sc.
Rnd 2: Ch 2, hdc2tog in same sc, ch 1, skip 1 sc, (hdc3tog in same sc, ch 1, skip 1 sc) around, ending with 1 sl st into 1st hdc cl.
Rnd 3: Ch 1, (1 sc in hdc cl, 1 sc around c) around, ending with 1 sl st into 1st sc.
Rnd 4: Ch 1 and then work 1 crab st in each sc around.
On the candle holder cover, also work the edging around bottom edge.

Yarn Information

Dale Garn yarns are available from:
Dale Garn North America
www.dalegarnnorthamerica.com

DROPS Garn Studio yarns are available from:
Garn Studio
www.garnstudio.com

Du Store Alpakka yarns may be purchased (with international shipping charges) from:
Knitting with Attitude
www.knitwithattitude.com

Lang yarns are available from a variety of stockists internationally, as listed at:
Lang Yarns
www.langyarns.com

Rauma yarns are available from:
The Yarn Guys
www.theyarnguys.com

Sandnes yarns may be purchased (with international shipping charges) from:
Scandinavian Knitting Design
www.scandinavianknittingdesign.com

A variety of additional and substitute yarns are available from:
Webs – America's Yarn Store
75 Service Center Road
Northampton, MA 01060
800-367-9327
www.yarn.com

LoveKnitting.com
www.loveknitting.com/us

If you are unable to obtain any of the yarn used in this book, it can be replaced with a yarn of a similar weight and composition. Please note, however, the finished projects may vary slightly from those shown, depending on the yarn used. Try www.yarnsub.com for suggestions.

For more information on selecting or substituting yarn, contact your local yarn shop or an online store; they are familiar with all types of yarns and would be happy to help you. Additionally, the online knitting community at Ravelry.com has forums where you can post questions about specific yarns. Yarns come and go so quickly these days and there are so many beautiful yarns available.

Acknowledgments

Thank you to Tina at the yarn shop Tjorven for help with the yarn—but also because she put me in contact with Tine Solheim. It was then that this endeavor became serious! Via Tine, I was introduced to several people in the industry, including at Cappelen Damm, with this book as the end result.

A big thank you to everyone at Cappelen Damm, especially Toril Blomqvist, Kaja Marie Kvernbakken, and last but certainly not least Inger Margrethe Karlsen, for wonderful support, smart tips, and positive attitudes.

Guri Pfeifer took the loveliest photos, and I'm so grateful! Thanks also to the models Siri Brattås, Martine Aspenes, and Anniken Røkke Bergli with sweet Hippie, for displaying my designs in the best possible way.

Lise Mosveen, who arranged the interior photos and text—it was a treat to see the book come together.

Thanks to Grete Holter for help with crocheting three of the cardigans, and thanks to Zsuzsa Hortolányi, who helped me in the summer when I was at the cabin and realized I really didn't have time to crochet the rest of the garments by myself!

I also want to thank my beloved husband and my dear son, who did so much so I had time to do what I most like to do! Thanks to Du Store Alpakka, Rauma Ullvarefabrikk, and Sandnes Garn for their contributions and support.

Abbreviations and Terms

beg	begin(s)(ing)	in	inch(es)
BO	bind off (= British cast off)	mm	millimeters
BP	back post	pm	place marker
ch	chain	rem	remain(s)(ing)
cl	cluster	rep	repeat(s)
cm	centimeter(s)	rnd(s)	round(s)
CO	cast on	RS	right side
dc	double crochet (= British treble crochet)	sc	single crochet (= British double crochet)
dc2tog	work 2 double crochet sts together = 1 st decreased	sc2tog	work 2 single crochet sts together = 1 st decreased
dtr	double treble (= British quadruple treble)—begin with 3 wraps around hook	sl	slip
est	established	st(s)	stitch(es)
FP	front post	tog	together
g	grams	tr	treble (= British double treble)
gr	group	WS	wrong side
hdc	half double crochet (= British half treble)		
hdc2tog	work 2 half double crochet sts together = 1 st decreased		

crab stitch: single crochet worked from left to right

[ ] brackets enclose a repeat that includes sections in ( ) repeated within the larger repeat or pattern

( ) parentheses enclose a repeat

* - * + ** - ** used to indicate the beginning and end of a series of repeats